CW00858227

sport

dedication

For Miranda and Bridie.

thegoodwebguide

sport

Philip Barton

The Good Web Guide Limited • London

First Published in Great Britain in 2001 by The Good Web Guide Limited
Broadwall House, 21 Broadwall, London, SE1 9PL

www.thegoodwebguide.co.uk

Email:feedback@thegoodwebguide.co.uk

10 9 8 7 6 5 4 3 2 1

A catalogue record for this book is available from the British Library.

ISBN 1-903282-071

Project Editor Michelle Clare

Design by Myriad Creative Ltd

Printed in Italy at LEGO S.p.A.

contents

the good web guides

The World Wide Web is a vast resource, with millions of sites on every conceivable subject, where cyber-communities have grown, and people have formed relationships, and even married on the net.

However, busy people want to use the internet for quick access to information, rather than spending hours on end surfing; it can be a quick and useful resource if you are looking for specific information.

The Good Web Guides have been published with this in mind, and to give you a head start in your search, our researchers have come up with a collection of reviews of the best sites around.

Our recommendation is impartial ; reviews are focused on the website and what it sets out to do, rather than an endorsement of a company, or their product. A small but beautiful site run by a one-man band may be rated higher than an ambitious but flawed site run by a mighty organisation.

Relevance to the UK-based visitor is also given a high premium: tantalising as it is to read about purchases you can make in California, because of delivery charges, import duties and controls it may not be as useful as a local site.

Our reviewers considered a number of questions when reviewing the sites, such as: How quickly do the sites and individual pages download? Can you move around the site easily and get back to where you started, and do the links work? Is the information up to date and accurate? And is the site pleasing to the eye and easy to read? More importantly, we also asked whether the site has something distinctive to offer. On the basis of the answers to these questions, sites are given ratings out of five. As we aim only to include sites that we feel are of serious interest, there are very few low-rated sites.

Remember: the collection of reviews you see here is just a snapshot of the sites at a particular time. The process of choosing and writing about sites is rather like painting the Forth Bridge: as each section appears complete, new sites are launched and others are modified.

As this is the first edition of the Good Web Guide, all our sites have been reviewed by the author and research team, but we'd like to know what you think. Contact us via the website or email feedback@thegoodwebguide.co.uk. You are welcome to recommend sites, quibble about the ratings, point out changes and inaccuracies or suggest new features to assess.

You can find us at www.thegoodwebguide.co.uk

introduction

When I was first invited to write this book, I admit that I wondered whether there were going to be enough good sports sites to fill even half of the following pages. I also worried that I might be drawn into a virtual world of sporting nuts and cranks, who would berate me with their views on their favourite team or player until I slumped on my computer beaten and tearful. How wrong I was on both counts. There are some great sports sites out there, ranging from the sophisticated, all singing and dancing offerings of mighty media corporations, to the niche operation of a fan. And the marvellous thing about the internet is that these two types of site can rub shoulders effortlessly, and be reached with just the same ease. All you need is a computer with a modem, a phone line, and an Internet Service Provider.

As I researched the book, I also began to realise that it is through sports websites that the true massive potential of the internet as a medium can be tapped. Certainly, in the sites that offer multi-media content, such as radio and video clips, as well as text and still photos, you can see that we are only a few steps away from a really exciting media convergence. In some ways, sport was almost made for the internet. In the not too distant future, I am sure we will be able to watch live webcasts of Premiership football, or top cricket and rugby, on an affordable pay per view basis. With the added bonus of watching the post-match press conference, replaying the highlights, and downloading pages of statistics and pre- and post-match analysis.For the moment though, the speed of data transfer from dial-up ISP's makes trying to watch even short video clips a frustrating experience. The best that can really be achieved with even a 56kbps connection is a sort of slide show with commentary, but the arrival of broadband technology will surely change all that.

Finally, I have a few apologies to make. I am sorry if you have bought this book, hoping to find a review of your favourite club or player's site. There are some magnificent sites out there, particularly from football clubs, but I figured that if you were a fan you would probably find your own way there anyway. I was also probably more likely to alienate more sports fans by the sites that I omitted than delight others by the ones that I included. If you need directions to your club's site you will find them at then end of the chapters on football, cricket and rugby.

And last of all, I apologise if your favourite site has not been included. I looked at around a thousand sites before selecting the hundred or so that have made into the Good Web Guide, and the ultimate criteria were that the site had to have a great idea or to have great content, or both. It is always possible though in the fast moving world of the web that I may have missed a corker. Let me know if you think I have.

Philip Barton, February 2001

acknowledgements

Many thanks to: Michelle Clare and Kevin Harley for their encouragement, meticulous checking and keeping me on the straight and narrow; Elaine Collins for her enthusiasm for this project; Miranda Blum for her ever reliable advice; and Nicky Granville for thinking of me in the first place.

user key

£	subscription required
R	registration required
🔒	secure online ordering
UK	country of origin

general sports sites

sport

overall rating:	★★★★★
classification:	news, results, comment
updated:	frequently
navigation:	★★★★★
readability:	★★★★★
readability:	★★★★★
speed:	★★★★★
UK	

www.news.bbc.co.uk/sport
BBC Online

The BBC have produced a gem of a website here, which oozes class and is a byword for speed and reliability. The BBC's vast network of correspondents and strong editing ensures a high quality of writing, and the columnists are particularly well informed. The Audio/Video reports are similarly extensive with a good quality of video even with a 56k connection to RealPlayer. This is not the site for you if you are a stats addict though – the emphasis is very much on news reporting and the statistics sections tend to be limited.

The design is fresh and readable with a particularly good use of photographs to illustrate the stories. Navigation is a joy. There is a clear main menu on the left of the screen, stories in the centre and links to special sections on the right. If you do get lost, then there is a reminder called You Are In... just below the titles, which tells you exactly where you are within the site.

SPECIAL FEATURES

Audio /Video has lots of up-to-date audio football reports and post-match interviews with managers and players. The most recent of these can be found in Hot Quotes. There is also information on which football matches will be available on Live Webcast commentary. Finally, you can listen to an audio update of all the sporting action in SOL (Sport Online) Daily. You will need a copy of RealPlayer for all of these services.

In Depth contains feature sections on the really big sporting stories of the moment, which at the time of writing ranged from Corruption in Cricket to the career of Lennox Lewis. These sections often contain some interactive elements and use a wide spectrum of contributors to explore the subject. This is also a good area if you want to catch up on what happened at the major events in the year, such as Wimbledon, the home Test Series, or the Open golf.

Sports Talk is subtitled Have Your Say Today, and is a well-managed forum on hot (mainly football) subjects. You can send in your email thoughts to be added to the threads raised by the BBC sports team. There are also sections for all of the English and Scottish Leagues, including an intriguing area where fans make an assessment about who might win their team's league.

Photo Galleries contains all the latest football action, posted very quickly on the day of the matches, as well as coverage of all the other major sporting events going on around the world.

Football may not have much in the way of statistics but it has a match reporting network in place that can only be the envy of other sports websites. Here you can read succinct accounts of the action from every match in every professional league in England and Scotland, as well as the English Conference. There is also a Saturday afternoon service, where you can watch the action unfold 'minute-by-minute' from all of the Premiership matches. The My Club section allows you to tailor news, reports and statistics for the club of your choice.

There are comprehensive sections too on the Champions League, the Uefa Cup, World Cup 2002, Serie A from Italy, and the Primera Liga of Spain.

The online columnists include David Lawrenson and Gordon Smith, the BBC's Scottish Premier League expert. Finally, if you are pining for 'the voice' of football you can listen to James Alexander Gordon intoning the results in time-honoured fashion.

Cricket contains all of the news and scores from around the counties, including a 'live' scoreboard and scorecard when play is in progress. There are also interviews (some of them in audio) with the top names of the moment, as well as a round-up service in Cricket in Brief, and stats from the 2000 season.

The Cricket section features have lots of interviews with current and ex-players (again often in audio or video), and reports from the BBC's journalists such as Pat Murphy or Jonathan Agnew. Aggers is also available to answer your questions if you send them in on an email.

Rugby Union has news, results, fixtures and standings from the domestic and European action. At the time of writing the In Depth section also had a special area for the Welsh/Scottish League, and lots of detail on the Welsh game can be found by following the link called scrumv. If you can't see this link then go direct to www.bbc.co.uk/wales/scrumv/.

The BBC's Rugby Union columnists include Eddie Butler, Alastair Hignell, John Beattie and Graham Thomas. There is also a section called Diprose's Diary, where current player Tony Diprose gives his view of events from Saracens.

Rugby League was devoted to the Rugby World Cup 2000, at the time of writing, with some limited close of season news from the domestic scene. RWC coverage had all of the news, fixtures and results, as well as a venue guide, photo galleries, audio/video interviews, and columns from England's Kris Radlinski and Wales's Anthony Sullivan. There were also links to Live Webcast commentaries on big games.

Tennis has tournament news and results and rankings for the Top 20 men and women players. There is also a column from Iain Carter, audio interviews, and a strong section on UK tennis, including updates on recent initiatives from the LTA.

Golf contains results and rankings, video and audio interviews with players from the press room of major tournaments, and a section on Golf in the UK.

Motorsport has Audio/Video reports from the latest events plus some special features such as a History of Ferrari. There are columns from Jonathan Legard and Suzi Perry, and a comprehensive results section for 4 Wheels, 2 Wheels, International and Domestic events.

Athletics has plenty of results, fixtures and in-depth reports, such as the latest developments in the fight against doping in the sport. At the time of writing, there were also good sections rounding up all the action from the 2000 Olympics and Paralympics.

Other Sports has latest news items from minority sports, such as Boxing, Snooker, Horse Racing, Basketball, Ice Hockey, Gymnastics, Cycling and Baseball.

Results/Fixtures has a round up of all the results from around the world, split up into individual sports or collated together. If you want 'live' ticker scoring, then you can click the link called Launch Desktop Scorecard.

OTHER FEATURES

If you want opinion, go straight to BBC Pundits, which collates all the recent articles from the BBC's impressive set of columnists. More light-hearted chat can be found in Funny Old Game, which has a refreshingly scurrilous column from Derek 'Robbo' Robson - 'the notorious Tees Mouth of Radio Five Live'.

An extremely classy news reporting machine, which is just about as quick and reliable as sport on the web gets.

www.ananova.com/sports/
Ananova Limited from the Press Association

Ananova already supply sports news content to many of the big, well-established sports websites, so if you like your news raw and very, very fast, then this site is for you. There are, however, very few extra frills in the way of photographs or stats, which makes Ananova really for the newshound only.

The design is dominated by an animated, computer generated, female newsreader, who is the personification of Ananova. The text design is clean and readable. Navigation is fairly simple. You can access the main areas of the site via a main menu on the left of the screen. Special sections are in red, the remainder in green.

SPECIAL FEATURES

Video is where Ananova reads the news of the sports highlights. She has a rather alarming, metallic, American accented voice, but once you have got used to that, she provides a good round up and lively commentary with still pictures. You will need RealPlayer to use this service.

Alerts can be found in the main menu just below the titles. Here you can make request for email news to be sent to your desktop or to your WAP phone, with the added bonus of being able to narrow down your areas of interest to a very fine degree.

| overall rating: |
| ★ ★ ★ ★ |

| classification: |
| news, results |

| updated: |
| frequently |

| navigation: |
| ★ ★ ★ ★ |

| contents: |
| ★ ★ ★ ★ ★ |

| readability: |
| ★ ★ ★ ★ |

| speed: |
| ★ ★ ★ ★ ★ |

| UK |

OTHER FEATURES

Football is by far the largest section, and allows you to search for news by team, view full match reports, watch a live scores ticker, or simply catch up with fixtures, results and tables for the four English and Scottish League Divisions.

Cricket has live scores and scorecards, as well as all of the news, tables and averages.

Rugby Union is searchable by English Division, European competition, Welsh/Scottish League, Six Nations, Welsh Divisions or Scottish Divisions.

Rugby League had a very full section on the Rugby World Cup at the time of writing.

Motorsport is divided into sections for Rally, CART, Touring Cars and there are separate sections for F1 and Superbikes.

The other sections tend to provide a straight news service but there are plenty of sports to choose from. You will find all the latest stories from Tennis, Golf, Athletics, Cycling, Boxing, Horse Racing, Snooker, Darts, American Football and Basketball. Minority sports sections can be found via the Sport Directory in the main menu. There are pages for Baseball, Darts, Finswimming, Hockey, Ice Hockey, Rowing, Sailing, Skiing, Squash, Swimming, Xtreme and Yachting.

A great resource for any sports fan who likes their news fresh and first. Well written, snappy stories from right across the sporting spectrum.

www.sky.com/sports/home
BSkyB

As one would expect, this is a very slick news and results service with plenty of video and pundit spin-offs from Sky Sports TV. The emphasis is very much on football though, and the coverage of less popular sports is often not much more than a pure news and results service.

The site has a neat design and a clear main menu on the left of the screen. It is worth noting, however, that once you are in a section, the more unusual features tend to be in highlighted sections in a menu on the right of the screen.

SPECIAL FEATURES

Football The most interesting sections are on the menu on the right of the screen. Here you can read Steve Claridge's comments on Division One in Nationwide View, Jimmy Hill's thoughts in The Last Word (this can also be accessed via the TV section in the main menu) or email Andy Gray your football questions in Ask Andy. Also in the TV section is Pitchside, containing the thoughts of touchline reporter Clare Tomlinson.

While matches are in progress, you can see scores as they happen in Gillette Soccer Special. There is also a round up of tales from the tabloids in What the Papers Say, a chance to vote for your Save of the Month, and some bite-sized Opta Stats (see p.67 for more about how these statistics are compiled).

overall rating:
★ ★ ★ ★

classification:
news, results, comment

updated:
frequently

navigation:
★ ★ ★ ★

contents:
★ ★ ★ ★ ★

readability:
★ ★ ★ ★

speed:
★ ★ ★

UK

The rest of the Football section is devoted to a very slick news and statistics service, with the added bonus of viewing video clips of post-match manager and player interviews. These clips can also be accessed via the Video section in the main menu – you will need Windows Media Player to watch.

The Football homepage has headline news and reports from the most recent matches. News articles, results and fixtures are searchable for every club in the English and Scottish Leagues. There are additional sections for Premier League Clubs in England, and Rangers and Celtic in Scotland. Here you can find Squad Stats, Club Info and History, Photo Action, and for some clubs the chance to Ask The Expert (a local journalist) about the fortunes of your team. There is also an archive of Premiership match reports.

There are lots of England reports and features in International, a Spanish League round up in La Liga, and a big archive of match reports and results in World Cup, AXA FA Cup, Worthington Cup and Women's Football. All the football action coming up on Sky can be found in TV.

Video houses an extensive selection of clips, containing both live action and reaction for Football, Boxing, Cricket, Golf, Rugby League and Rugby Union. You can also listen to a brief sports news bulletin in this section from Sky Sports Radio. The bulletin is updated four times a day. Windows Media Player is required. Some of the other sports covered on this site have feature sections, which go beyond the usual news, fixtures and results service. These can all be found in the menu on the right of the screen within the relevant sections. In Cricket, Bob Willis or

David Lloyd will answer your email questions in Caught & Bowled. Rugby Union emails will be answered by Stuart Barnes in Under The Posts. There is a weekly column in Rugby League by Mike Stephenson called Stevo Says and a weekly Basketball column by Andy Cadle titled Cadle's Corner.

OTHER FEATURES

Cricket has useful Fixtures, Results and tour itineraries, as well as domestic Tables, Test Averages, and Test and ODI rankings. There is also a photo archive and Pen Pics of current England players.

Rugby Union and **Rugby League** have Headlines, Results and Fixtures with additional squad and statistical information for the Premier Rugby Union clubs.

Tennis contains Reports, Headlines, Features and Interviews with additional sections on the four Grand Slam tournaments.

Golf has sections on the Euro Tour and the US Tour, as well as Headlines, Scores, Rankings and a small features section.

Boxing contains Headlines, Results and a Features section which concentrates on the heavyweight division.

Motorsport has News, Schedules, Results and Standings for Formula 1, Superbikes, Moto GP, Rallying, Speedway, NASCAR and CART.

US Sport has the same information for NFL, NBA, NHL, Major League Baseball and Major League Soccer.

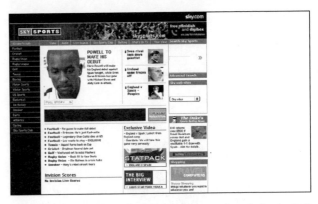

There are more British results, stats and standings in Basketball and Ice Hockey. While Snooker contains headlines, schedules /results, rankings and top player profiles.

Athletics and Darts are links to www.onrunning.com and www.planetdarts.com respectively, and the Sailing section contains a selection of relevant links.

Games has Fantasy games with cash prizes for Football, Golf and Formula 1.

A slick, professional site with a strong football bias.

www.sportinglife.com
Sporting Life

Sportinglife.com (part of the Trinity Mirror Group and the Press Association) is a solid, dependable general sports news site with an emphasis on betting. The site has particular strengths in its racing and football sections, and also has some good comment and editorial content.

The site has a bold style and is enjoyable to navigate. Clicking on any of the items in the main menu on the left screen opens up a sub-menu for that subject, which is also on the left of the screen. Just click on Home to get back to where you started when you have finished in a section.

SPECIAL FEATURES

Fanzine is where you'll find the thoughts of Sportinglife's columnists covering the sports spectrum and who include Neal Collins, Ben Mack and Grant Williams.

Bettingzone contains news, Odds, Statistics and Spreads for all of the major UK sports and some US ones. You will find Latest Previews and Latest Prices in the special features menu to the right of the screen. On the left, there are tips in Today's Bets and Life Saver, and a remarkably frank assessment of how those tips fared in Record.

Racing contains weekly audio previews of the week's racing from the outspoken John McCririck of Channel 4 fame. You will need a copy of RealPlayer to listen.

The Racing section also has news and interviews, a preview of The Day's Action, Race Cards and Live Betting Shows direct from the racecourse. In the Race Cards, you will find links to a horse's past record in other races, and links to how the jockeys and trainers have been faring this season. There are also Fixtures and Archives sections.

You can choose your Racing Results in a Fast or Full version, look at Season or 14 day Stats for Jump and Flat Trainers and Jockeys, follow the press tipsters' Nap form, or read comprehensive profiles of all the Courses in the UK. Stable Tours has interviews with the country's leading trainers.

Football is a very comprehensive section, with news, match reports, tables and stats for all of the English and Scottish Leagues, European competitions, European Leagues, Domestic Cups and the World Cup. These are searchable by your favourite Team in most cases. Live contains Latest Scores, Reports, Quotes and Tables, as well as a Vidiprinter for live scoring and goal flashes. Finally, there is information on Top Scorers, Transfers, Suspensions and Pools news.

OTHER FEATURES

All of the sections listed below have Betting News as well as headline news.

Cricket has full Scorecards and reports on current international and domestic matches, as well as Fixtures, Tables, Averages.

Rugby Union has Live Scores, Fixtures, Results, Reports and Tables, with the option of searching the above by Zurich Premiership Team.

Rugby League contains Profiles and Reports from Super League teams, as well as Live Scores and top Try and Goal Scorers. There was also a very full Rugby World Cup section at the time of writing.

Formula 1 has Live Action, Schedules, Results, Standings, Reports, useful Team and Driver Profiles, and comprehensive Driver and Constructor Statistics for the last five seasons.

Golf contains Scores, Money Lists and an Archive section on the Majors. Tennis has Results and Rankings. Boxing has News and reports on Big Fights. NFL has Schedules, Standings and Stats. The Snooker section contains Draws, Results, Profiles, Rankings and a Form Guide, and there is a round up of alternative action in Other Sports. Competitions provides the opportunity to win tickets to sporting events.

A wide-ranging sports news site with strong sections on racing, football and betting.

sport

overall rating:
★ ★ ★ ★

classification:
news, results, comment

updated:
frequently

navigation:
★ ★ ★

contents:
★ ★ ★ ★

readability:
★ ★ ★ ★

speed:
★ ★ ★ ★

UK

www.sports.com
The Sports.com Online Network

This is a lively sports news and comment site, which covers a fair range of sports in reasonable depth and has a good team of high-profile columnists on its books. There is also a strong football audio section containing both match reports and feature articles.

The site has a modern, bouncy style with plenty of photos to illustrate the stories. Navigation can be a little trying at times. The main sports menu lies across the top of the screen, but the left hand sub-menu within each section re-orders itself depending on your location. This can be a little disorientating.

SPECIAL FEATURES

AudioCentre can be found in the Football section and has a good selection of match reports and feature articles. You will need a copy of Windows Media Player before you can listen. Match commentary highlights are brought to you by Capital Gold's excitable Jonathan Pearce together with former player Tony Gale. There are also audio previews of the weekend's big games on Fridays, and a Midweek Focus feature programme, which explores topical issues with the help of pundits and current managers and players.

Elsewhere in the Football section, you can find a column from BBC pundit Mark Lawrenson. Football news is searchable by

English or Scottish League or Club, with additional sections for Transfers and Match Reports. There are also sections for the domestic Cups, Champions League, Uefa Cup and the major European Leagues, some of which contain match reports as well as scores and stats. Finally, there is a section for the World Cup qualifying campaign and a chance to look at This Week in Photos, although they proved rather slow to download.

Competitions can also be found in the Football section. You need to make a free registration first, but can then play a variety of prediction and fantasy manager games, all with cash prizes. Futbol Mondial is in Fan Zone and is a collection of football features from around the world.

OTHER FEATURES

Cricket contains a top columnist in the shape of the always opinionated Ian Botham. This section also has scoreboards, tour itineraries and news, which is searchable for all of the Test playing nations.

Golf's columnist is Chris Moody, a former European Tour pro. You will also find news, photos, Profiles of the top players, Rankings, money lists, and separate sections on both the Major Tournaments and famous Courses.

Tennis has news, results and Profiles of the top men and women players. There are also picture galleries searchable by player, and separate sections for Grand Slam, Masters Series and Davis Cup Tournaments.

Rugby Union contains an occasional column by Will Carling, the former England skipper. There are also all the news, results and fixtures from the Zurich Premiership with additional sections for the Six Nations, Super 12 and Tri-Nations.

Rugby League has a dedicated reporter in Keith McGhie, and contained a comprehensive section on the Rugby League World Cup at the time of writing.

F1 contains latest news, brief Team and Driver Profiles, Circuit descriptions and standings. There are also reports, stats and photos from every Grand Prix of the season.

Sailing has an in-depth section on the Swedish Match Grand Prix Sailing Tour, complete with Standings, Schedule and profiles of Skippers. There is also news coverage of other major races and a sailing TV Schedule.

Boxing has headlines, results and photos from top bouts.

Tips contains a sub-section called All The Odds, which makes a comparison of online bookmakers prices for Asian Handicaps, UK Football, Euro Football, Cricket, Golf and Rugby. You can also have your email betting questions answered in Flutter's Feedback, or subscribe to various tip sheets. Finally, you can look at pictures of pretty girls in swimsuits in Models.

Shopping can be found in the menu on the left of the screen in any of the main sports sections. Here you can buy football shirts, gifts, kids items, coaching aids and collectibles, or visit the dedicated Man Utd shop. Cricket has videos, apparel and photos. Rugby has shirts. Golf contains bags, clubs, balls and

shoes. F1 has apparel and NFL has shirts and jerseys. There is also a Books and Video store. Some items have free UK delivery but others contain charges.

Finally, if your language skills are up to it, you can see what the sporting world looks like in Sports.com sister sites in Singapore, Korea, France, Germany, Italy, Spain and the USA.

A lively site with some big name columnists.

sport

overall rating: ★★★	

classification:
news, results, videos

updated:
frequently

navigation:
★★★

contents:
★★★

readability:
★★★

speed:
★★★

UK

www.eurosport.com
Eurosport

Eurosport cover a very wide range of sports in this website but are at their strongest in their sections on Motorsport, Cycling, Wintersports, Tennis and Athletics.

The style of the site is fresh with some bold colours and lots of photos but overall the pages tend to be a little too cluttered and busy. Navigating the homepage via main menu in the top right of the screen is simple enough but the content of individual sports sections can be confusing with competing menus on both sides of the page.

SPECIAL FEATURES

Motorsport can be reached by clicking on Formula 1 or Rally, where you will also find sections on Moto GP and SBK. These sections have the usual results and standings services combined with a great range of video and audio interviews. The Le Mans and Paris-Dakar-Cairo sections also have very good video highlights packages, and there are occasional special video reports from such events as a Ferrari Testing session. You will need a copy of RealPlayer before you can watch.

Cycling has some superbly detailed coverage of Road, Track and Mountain Bike Racing. The Road section is particularly full with sections on the World Cup, Giro, Tour de Suisse, Vuelta and the World Championships. However, Eurosport really pull out the stops with their coverage of the Tour de France. There are detailed reports from every stage, profiles of Teams and Riders, and live radio coverage from Radio Tour. RealPlayer is again required. The Track section covers the World Track Championships and has Portraits of the top stars, and the World Championships are also covered in Mountain Biking.

Wintersports contains an excellent Alpine Skiing section. Here you can find results and standings from all of the different events, a searchable database of skiers, video highlights of races, and some great video interveiws with the top performers in Star Corner. Wintersports also has sections on Ski Jumping, Biathlon, Snowboarding and Bobsleigh.

Tennis boasts a comprehensive News and results service for Current Tournaments, and some exclusive video reports on top players in Star Corner. There are also special sections on the Grand Slam tournaments and The Davis Cup, and some brief profiles of Players.

Athletics has reports from the Golden League, Grand Prix, World Championships and Indoor Championships. There is also a Records section and profiles of top Athletes, although these tend not to be very well written. There are, however, many interesting Video interviews with some of the world's best performers.

News Live! has all the latest headlines straight off the news wire plus live text commentary from the day's bigger sporting events.

Clicking on the Audio/Video button in the main menu is a quick way of getting to all the latest video or audio highlights, features and interviews. RealPlayer is required.

OTHER FEATURES

Football has new results, fixtures and tables for the top two divisions in the English, German, French, Italian and Spanish leagues. There are also sections on the various Cup competitions, European competitions and the respective National Teams. Finally, you can get results and tables information for every country in Europe not already mentioned.

Rugby contains news, fixtures and results from the respective top leagues in England and France, as well as audio interviews and text commentary on the big European Cup and Shield games. There are also sections on World Cup '99, the Six Nations and Super Twelve.

Other Sports has a drop-down menu leading to a section on Cricket with reports from around the world.

Golf has news and scores coverage for the European, USPGA, Euroladies and LPGA Tours. There are separate sections for the Majors and the Ryder Cup with Live Text Commentary when the tournaments are in progress.

Olympic Games has news items plus retrospectives from Sydney 2000.

Sailing contains headline news from the big, current regattas.

Xtreme Sports leads to a youth and extreme sports area with text and video reports on Boarder X, Skier X, Half Pipe Snow and Half Pipe Ski.

The Game Zone has a variety of fantasy Management, Prediction and Trivia Quizzes for prizes, as well as a section called Adnatura Spirit, where you can submit your Dream Expedition Project in the hope of winning sponsorship for it.

Community has Chat and Forum areas and a chance to vote for the SportStar Awards, while Services offers a free, daily email newsletter.

Shopping has links to www.amazon.com and www.kitbag.com, as well as other sports merchandising and ticketing sites.

Wide ranging but variable sports coverage.

sport

overall rating: ★ ★ ★	

overall rating:
★ ★ ★

classification:
news, results, statistics

updated:
frequently

navigation:
★ ★ ★ ★ ★

contents:
★ ★ ★

readability:
★ ★ ★

speed:
★ ★ ★

UK

www.sportal.co.uk
The Sportal Network

Sportal are impressive for their wide-ranging European sports news service, and have good UK Football, Horseracing, Formula 1 and Tennis sections. As a whole, though, Sportal tends to lack the in-depth comment and feature articles that might set it apart from its competitors. The design is vibrant and easy on the eye. Navigation has been very well thought out, with a clear main menu on the left of the screen and equally clear sub-section headings.

SPECIAL FEATURES

Football contains a fine statistical service. Premiership clubs can be searched for Form, scorer Strike Rates, League Positions in a graphical format, charts of when goals are scored and conceded, and determination stats. These statistics are also available for the top clubs in France, Germany, Spain and Italy.

Clubs has all the results, fixtures and tables plus squad details with good Player biographies.

Results contains all of the match facts and Fixtures has Previews of Premiership matches. You can access News, Fixtures, Results and Tables for the Nationwide League, Scotland, Europe, Champions League and Uefa Cup. The England team section again has particularly good biographies.

Fanzone has Chat, Screensavers, a Trivia Quiz, Puzzles, and the opportunity to subscribe to a free, weekly email Newsletter.

Football Homepage is where you can find footie columns from Sky TV's Martin Tyler and Channel 4's Italian expert James Richardson.

Horseracing has some interesting Profiles of the top jockeys and trainers, and potted histories of every one of the Racecourses in the country. There is a good series of interviews with racing's movers and shakers in Trainer States in the News section, as well as tips from Sports Adviser and the Sportal staff.

Racing Today contains full cards from all of the meetings. There is also a Results service and a glossary of racing terms in Beginners Guide. The Betting section is a link to Coral Eurobet.

Formula 1 has previews, biographies and photo galleries in Drivers & Teams, and track profiles and snappy race reports in Circuit Calendar. The Paddock Life section contains gossip and news from beyond the race track and Pit Lane has Chat, Competitions and a email Newsletter service.

OTHER FEATURES

Tennis has very brief biographies of the top 20 men and women Players, and a full news, results and fixtures service. You can listen to post-match player interviews (RealPlayer required) from selected Grand Slam tournaments in Media Centre, or search for photos of your favourite player in Photo Galleries. The Fanzone has a Trivia Quiz and Screensavers to download.

Golf also has brief player biographies, plus News, Rankings and a Photo Gallery. The Media Centre contains audio player interviews from the 2000 USPGA tournament (RealPlayer) but the Leaderboard link was not working at the time of writing, despite a big tournament in progress.

Cricket contains brief news from the England camp, plus links to rather fuller Australian and South African sections.

Rugby Union is a link to www.scrum.com (see p153) and Rugby League is a link to www.playtheball.com (see p157).

Finally, clicking through to Sportal.com will provide sports headlines for Germany, Italy, France, Spain, Denmark, Sweden, Australia and South Africa.

A strong football section cannot disguise the fact that a lot of Sportal's sports coverage lacks real depth.

OTHER SITES OF INTEREST

Rivals
www.rivals.net
Rivals is predominantly a host site for a family of independent, fan-based sports sites, with a small amount of editorial of their own. On Rivals you will find a network of more than 300 sites, although only one independent fan site from each team, sport or personality is allowed. The editors are all genuine fans of the teams they report on and you can find sites for Football League teams, County Cricket, Professional Rugby, Formula One, Cycling, Rallying and Other (minority) Sports.Rivals is certainly worth checking out if you are tired of the official line and want some more independent comment about your team or club.

chapter 2
cricket

official sites

overall rating:
★ ★ ★ ★ ★

classification:
news, scores, comment

updated:
scores every 60 seconds

navigation:
★ ★ ★ ★ ★

contents:
★ ★ ★ ★ ★

readability:
★ ★ ★ ★ ★

speed:
★ ★ ★ ★

UK

www.ecb.co.uk
England and Wales Cricket Board and Cricinfo

The England and Wales Cricket Board have joined together with Cricinfo to produce a truly excellent website. As with other Cricinfo sites, it is a joy to navigate. Content appears in the middle of the screen, and a menu on the left leads you smoothly around the site. For news, information and comment, this site provides a comprehensive resource for the English cricket fan. The multimedia elements add an extra level of gloss to an already superb package.

SPECIAL FEATURES

Cricket Channel and **Audio Commentary** push this website way ahead of the competition by providing a genuine multi-media experience. Both these sections require a free download of RealPlayer from www.real.com but are well worth the trouble. The Cricket Channel provides both audio interviews and video clips of players and officials. Audio Commentary has real time match commentary from such luminaries as Ralph Dellor, Jack Bannister, Neil Foster and Tony Cozier.

Live Scores is Cricinfo's results service, with scorecard information updated every 60 seconds. Scores for all the first class games in the country are available in County Scoreboard.

There is also a Desktop Scorecard for abbreviated updates. News & Views provides in-depth coverage of all the latest from both the professional and amateur game.

International has a comprehensive round-up of all the scores, news and comment from England's current campaigns, plus a list of international fixtures in Index of All Tours.

Domestic leads you to The Counties, a superb resource for the domestic game. Clicking on an individual county takes you to in-depth news and views and contact information for your favourite team, or you can take a link straight to a county's official website. News and information on the women's game is available in Women's Cricket. In addition, you can help the ECB

achieve its goal of an archive of every cricket club in the UK by registering your club in Directory.

Fan's Centre has a fun Fantasy game, incorporating both the Test and County seasons. Worth a Shout gives you the chance to air your views about topical issues, and Mail the Team allows you to send a personal message to a current England international player. You can also Chat Live, as well as catching up on TV & Radio listings and Ticket Availability for international matches.

Deep Extra Cover takes you to Play the Game, an invaluable resource for anybody, young or old, who is thinking of taking up cricket. The website's stats section is also within Deep Extra Cover, and is largely a mirror of Cricinfo's other statistical sections with an English bias. Still, once you have explored StatsGuru, Statistics, Scorebook, Player Profiles, and Grounds, there is little or nothing that you won't know about English cricket.

OTHER FEATURES

There is a massive selection of internet links.

A hugely impressive website, which complements Cricinfo's other sites with seamless efficiency.

news sites

www-uk.cricket.org
Cricinfo

This is simply one of the best sports web sites around. Cricinfo is so comprehensive and so well thought-out that it makes all other cricket sites virtually superfluous. Cricinfo's key strength is that it caters for all lovers of cricket, from the dizzy heights of the international touring circuit down to the lowliest village club. Compared with other sites, the depth and breadth of coverage is dazzling. It is even more impressive, then, that this site is so easy to navigate. Latest news appears in the middle of the screen, scoreboards and interactive on the right, and the main menu on the left. And because Cricinfo hosts so many of the official sites around the world, it is always easy to get back to the homepage if you get lost in a backwater.

SPECIAL FEATURES

Official Sites for all of the Test Playing Nations and the ICC Associate and Affiliate Members can be found by clicking on the flags at the top of the screen, or by clicking Official Sites and clicking the relevant logo. All of these sites are hosted by Cricinfo too; so, although each nation's site has a distinctive feel, they also have the same easily digestible format, with a mixture of results, scorecards and topical feature articles. From Official Sites you can also access a handful of sites for First Class

overall rating:
★ ★ ★ ★ ★

classification:
news, info, commerce

updated:
scores every 60 seconds

navigation:
★ ★ ★ ★ ★

contents:
★ ★ ★ ★ ★

readability:
★ ★ ★ ★ ★

speed:
★ ★ ★ ★

UK

sport

Teams, Cricket Associations and numerous British-based Cricket Societies from the Cheltenham Cricket Society to the Wombwell Cricket Lovers' Society.

Series provides links to in-depth information on the squads and the state of play in current Test series anywhere in the world. Domestic is a round-up of who is up and who is down in the first class game across the globe. There is also an archive section here in Test Series Summary and ODI Series/Tournament Summary, with a wealth of information on the outcome of matches between 1991 and 1999. Future Series gives calendar information on upcoming touring itineraries.

Latest is Cricinfo's news service, featuring scorecard information for all the first class games in the country available in Live Coverage. The scorecards are updated every 60 seconds, so you need barely miss a ball. And for real stats addicts, you can see the progress of a batsman's innings and a bowler's spell down to the last delivery. You can even tell who is facing whom in real time. The English County Scoreboard lets you keep simultaneous tabs on all the games throughout the country. News Articles provides in-depth comment on the game throughout the world, with the British content provided primarily by the Electronic Telegraph. Women's cricket is represented by a news, scores and features service in the Women section.

Live provides an opportunity to listen to ball-by-ball commentary on selected games. International matches are given preference but when there are none playing, ex-BBC man Ralph Dellor can pop up anywhere around the country. You will, though, need to download RealPlayer from www.real.com.

Cricinfo365 is a free Email service, delivering a daily digest of news, scores and comments to your desktop.

Cricshop offers you the chance to browse through a virtual gallery of cricket videos, books, and equipment, and to buy on-line through a secure connection. The Special Offers section has a good range of gifts and memorabilia for the cricket enthusiast. You can also search the shop if you want to narrow your search for a more specific item.

Database is a massive resource of cricket Pictures, Statistics and Archives, including scorecards for every test match ever played and an almost complete international first class archive from 1993 onwards. The StatsGuru is there to help you refine your search for the playing records and potted biographies of any player who has ever played international cricket. You can also find the great cricketing Articles in the Archives, trivia in the Statistics section and a comprehensive list of first class cricket Grounds. And if that wasn't enough, there is also a complete, up-to-date round-up of all the cricket Ratings in use around the world. Whatever method is used, Australia still seem to come out on top.

Interactive The Magazine, which is also known as Googler's Gazette, boasts 'random writings and original outbursts on the game we love'. It has some interesting articles from around the world by writers unusual to Britain, as well as a chance to make contributions yourself. There is also a Chat room, some fun Online Games, and some pre-arranged online Interviews with stars of the game. Cricket Carnival has more archived interviews and online coaching tips in the Net Session section. Polls allows

you to vote for your Man of the Match in all of the recent and current Tests and One Day Internationals. You need to register with Cricinfo before you can participate.

OTHER FEATURES

Cricket items can be bought and sold or swapped in the Classified section, Media tells you where current and upcoming tours will be broadcast, and About Cricket has all the laws of the game. Finally, Cricinfo has Links to over 2000 other cricket related sites.

A model for how sports websites should be, and a truly global scores, news and information service.

www.cricket4.com
Channel 4

Cricket 4 is designed to complement Channel 4's TV coverage but it has a lot to offer cricket fans, even when there isn't a domestic Test series in progress. In particular, there are some good pundits and a very sharp stats section.

The design is bright, clear and attractive and navigation could not be simpler. The main menu is at the top of the screen just below the titles and a sub menu opens, when appropriate, on the left of the relevant page.

SPECIAL FEATURES
Cricket 4's columnists are well worth reading and can be found within the News section of the main menu. Here you can catch up on the thoughts of Channel 4's front man, Mark Nicholas, plus the diaries of current England players Graham Thorpe and Michael Vaughan. You can expect a wider range of pundits when there is a Test series in progress in England.

Community has a high class message board where one of Channel 4's commentary team might break into the conversation to add a trenchant opinion or clear up that niggling dispute.

Statistics allows you to analyse test teams or individual players performances against a vast array of criteria. Here, Cricket 4 have added a neat twist with some snappy graphics, charts and

overall rating:	★ ★ ★ ★
classification:	news, scores, comment
updated:	regularly
navigation:	★ ★ ★ ★ ★
contents:	★ ★ ★ ★
readability:	★ ★ ★ ★
speed:	★ ★ ★ ★
UK	

graphs to get to an extra level of detail. A must if you want to know what percentage of Brian Lara's dismissals have been out caught, or if Andy Caddick performs better against the Pakistanis or the Kiwis.

World XI is a sophisticated, year-round fantasy management game with cricket prizes. It is free to register and play.

OTHER FEATURES

The Analyst section was still under construction at the time of writing but promises an online complement to Simon Hughes's look at the technical aspects of the game. It will also explain Channel 4's broadcasting innovations such as the Snickometer and the Red Zone.

News has some useful in-depth articles and breaking stories. International has all the current and recent news, scores and statistics from Tests and ODIs from all over the world.

Calendar allows you to take a daily, weekly, monthly or yearly look at upcoming international itineraries.

Email session reports is a free service allowing you to keep right on top of each and every international match.

An attractive site with some good pundits on board, well-presented stats, and a fun fantasy game.

www.cricketline.com
Cricketline from the 365 Network

Cricketline bills itself as 'The World's Ultimate Cricket Resource'. That mantle really belongs to Cricinfo, but Cricketline does have a lot to offer in a clear and uncluttered way. The site is a joy to navigate, with clear links to different areas on the left, news in the centre of the screen, and features on the right. The writing style is upbeat, fun, and likeably irreverent at times.

SPECIAL FEATURES

Features is one of this website's strongest areas. There is a good line-up of star cricketers, who are prepared to give some honest, hard-hitting views from inside the game. At the time of writing, Allan Donald and Viv Richards were penning regular articles. There are also some thought-provoking opinion pieces, written in a nicely irreverent style, from Cricketline's own writers.

On This Day is a fun service for trivia lovers. Cricketline scour the archives to find a famous cricketer – either from the past or present – with a birthday on today's date, and they then provide a jaunty outline of his career.

Statistics is a cleverly thought-out interactive package, where you can manipulate those stats in a mind-boggling variety of ways to determine which of the test teams really is the best side around. Funny that it still always seems to be Australia. There is even more detail to be had in the Players section, where you can pitch two giants of the game head-to-head to see how their

overall rating:	★ ★ ★ ★
classification:	news, scores
updated:	regularly throughout day
navigation:	★ ★ ★ ★ ★
contents:	★ ★ ★ ★
readability:	★ ★ ★ ★
speed:	★ ★ ★ ★
UK	

international careers match up.

Trivia has an addictive quiz where you can pit yourself against the clock and your chums to answer some tricky questions in the fastest possible time. Prizes are also available if you register to play.

OTHER FEATURES

Today's Games gives regular score updates for domestic and international cricket. Breaking News has the day's top stories. You can also get Free News via email in a daily, weekly, or preview-of-a-big-match form, as well as information on upcoming international fixtures, and a comprehensive results and match report service. Finally, there is more detail to be had about your favourite county and players in English Domestic, and an opportunity to air your views on Message Board.

A fun, less cluttered alternative to Cricinfo with enough information and statistics to satisfy most cricket fans.

www.cricketer.com
The Cricketer Magazine

This is mainly an electronic version of The Cricketer, a monthly magazine, with only a few fresh or original online features. It is a useful resource, though, for browsing through opinion pieces from hard-hitting columnists, and the Village Championship section gets right to the grass roots of the game.

SPECIAL FEATURES

Cricketer Championships is a comprehensive archive of all the Village Championship matches played since 1995, with a brief match report on each. You can also search for a specific team and track their progress through the competition.

On-Line Shop has a good range of items for sale, ranging from videos and books, to gift ideas, and clothing and equipment.

OTHER FEATURES

Regular Features gets you to Leader, an excellent way of checking out the opinions of some of the biggest names in the game, while Top Order has articles from the great and the good of cricket, the media and politics.

Not much interactivity in this site but the Village Championships section is a winner.

overall rating:	★ ★ ★
classification:	news, comment
updated:	daily
navigation:	★ ★ ★
contents:	★ ★ ★
readability:	★ ★ ★
speed:	★ ★ ★
UK	

sport

enthusiast sites

overall rating: ★ ★ ★ ★	
classification: news, comment, shopping	
updated: constantly	
navigation: ★ ★ ★ ★ ★	
contents: ★ ★ ★	
readability: ★ ★ ★ ★	
speed: ★ ★ ★	
UK	

www.cricnet.com
Professional Cricketers Association

Here's a site where you can almost smell the linseed oil. Cricnet claims to have been written by cricket fans for cricket fans, but it actually goes one better than that. It is written by professional cricket players for cricket fans, with the Professional Cricketers Association opening up the dressing room doors and letting the fans right inside. It's easy to navigate too, with a menu bar on the left, news in the centre, and special sections on the right.

SPECIAL FEATURES

County by County is where this site really scores. Here, a fan can get a genuinely unique insight into what motivates the professional players on the county circuit. For each match, the players write a Game Preview, a Game Report, and Stories as the match unfolds. There is also a no-holds-barred Venue section, where you can find out what the players think of some of the more far-flung cricket grounds on the County itinerary. The players don't claim to be professional writers, and not all of the pieces are elegantly written. But this is about as close as it is possible to get to the real atmosphere inside a dressing room.

Ball by Ball Coverage is an excellent, well-designed resource for the fan who wants up-to-date action delivered to the desktop.

Player Interviews is a great idea that seems a little underdeveloped as yet. There are one or two earthy and entertaining interviews about players by players, a small Where Are You Now? section about ex-players, and a player's view from around the world on the state of the international game. A few more pithy pieces about the heroes and the also-rans of the county scene would make this section fascinating reading. Test Update gives a player's insights into the state of the current England team, often picking up on small but important things that the pundits and commentators miss.

Cricnet Shop has a great range of items for sale, ranging from videos and books to gift ideas and clothing and equipment.

OTHER FEATURES

Today's Cricket has breaking news stories. Fixtures has forthcoming itineraries and Country vs Country is an international scorecard and match report service. Cricket History gives a potted evolution of the game, while Coaching has details of the PCA's work with youth development. Hall of Fame is the PCA's choice of the world's 50 greatest retired cricketers. Club Cricnet is a tool to tailor cricketing information interactively to an individual's requirements, but it is not up and running yet. There is a Bulletin Board on which you can air your views on the state of the game, plus the usual Stat Search service.

A great example of how the internet can bring the players and fans of a sport closer together. There should be more sports websites like this.

OTHER SITES OF INTEREST

England's Barmy Army
www.barmy-army.co.uk

The Barmy Army is a sort of unofficial supporters club for the England cricket team at home and abroad. Their stated aim is to 'make watching cricket more fun and much more popular', and they have won praise for their good-humoured and irrepressibly noisy approach to a catalogue of overseas England cricketing debacles. The website is simple but a great resource for any fan looking to travel to watch England abroad, and hoping to meet some like-minded companions when they get there. The website is at its best in offering tailor-made travel packages to England cricket matches all over the world. These can be found in the centre of the screen.

Wisden
www.wisden.com

Wisden, the most famous of cricket publishing names, was in the process of re-launching their website as this book went to press. Their previous website in association with The Guardian had some sharp writing, so it will certainly be worth checking back in mid-summer 2001 to see what there is on offer. In the meantime, Wisden have a temporary site, which has a few articles and a great section called Ask Steven. Here you can get all your obscure cricketing questions answered just by emailing Steven Lynch, Wisden's statistician-in-chief. Now there's no excuse for not knowing who made the most aggregate test runs without ever scoring a century. The new site promises news, scores and statistics in abundance.

First Class County Cricket Clubs – Official Websites

Derbyshire www.dccc.co.uk
Durham www.durham-ccc.org.uk
Essex www.essexcricket.org.uk
Glamorgan www-uk.cricket.org/link_to_
database/NATIONAL/ENG/FC_TEAMS/GLAM/
Gloucestershire www.glosccc.co.uk
Hampshire www-uk.cricket.org/link_to_
database/NATIONAL/ENG/FC_TEAMS/HANTS/
Kent www.kentcountycricket.co.uk
Lancashire www.lccc.co.uk
Leicestershire www.leicestershireccc.com
Middlesex www.middlesexccc.co.uk
Northamptonshire www.nccc.co.uk
Nottinghamshire www.trentbridge.co.uk
Somerset none at present
Surrey www.surreyccc.co.uk
Sussex www.sccc.demon.co.uk
Warwickshire warwickccc.org.uk
Worcestershire www.wccc.co.uk
Yorkshire www.yorkshireccc.org.uk

chapter 3
football

league sites by sponsors

www.football.nationwide.co.uk
FootballNOW!

Nationwide Building Society, the sponsors of the Football League, have produced a website here as solid and dependable as any Arsenal back four.

The design is crisp and clear and the content is an absolute mine of information, which should be enough to satisfy even the most die-hard fan of lower league football. The site is also very strong on photographs. Each top news story has an appropriate image, and there are lots of shots of players in action in the squad sections for each club.

Navigation is generally simple, although the series of drop-down menus which cascade down from the main menu on the left of the screen take a little getting used to, and require some deft mouse control. Another menu can be found running across the top of the screen, just below the main titles. This leads to areas in the site which are not specific to clubs or teams. The only disappointment in this site was the News Search section, an interactive tool for scouring news archives, which was not working at the time of writing.

overall rating:	★ ★ ★ ★
classification:	news, results, info
updated:	frequently
navigation:	★ ★ ★ ★
contents:	★ ★ ★
readability:	★ ★ ★ ★ ★
speed:	★ ★ ★ ★
UK	

sport

SPECIAL FEATURES

Nationwide League is located in the left-hand menu, and leads to a vast amount of well-ordered information, categorised first by Division and then by News, Fixtures, Results, Features, Tables, Stats, Teams and Fair Play.

Teams is the most useful section. Here you can catch up on all the latest news, results, fixtures and detailed match reports. Squad has potted biographical details on every player, and usually a photo of him in action. Pics has even more photos of your team, hopefully performing at their best. Teams also has a section called Football Fans Guide, which provides links to the club's official website, how to find the stadium, where to eat and drink just before you get there, and how much match tickets are going to set you back.

Nationwide Conference leads to a similar level of detail although there tends to be fewer photos.

The international scene is given the same sort of comprehensive treatment in England, Scotland and Wales, where you can find news, fixtures, results and squad details, not just on the Men's team but on Women's and Youth teams as well. England's Men's team has an additional section called Mr Hull's Diary, which brings you bulletins direct from the England training camp.

Other Football has its tongue firmly in cheek with regards to its name, and is where you can find News From the Premiership, covered in an impressive level of detail.

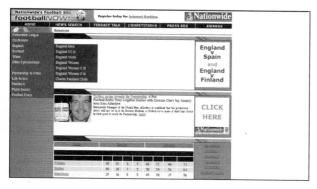

OTHER FEATURES

Fanfare is a chance for you to air your views about your club's season so far. The competitions have simple questions with prizes of tickets to top games. Awards has details of the managers and players of the month from the Nationwide League. TV listings can be found in Live Action.

An impressively full and easily accessible football resource. Equally good for finding out how your team is doing, checking up on the opposition, or planning your route to an away game.

sport

overall rating: ★ ★ ★ ★	
classification: e-zine, news, statistics	
updated: regularly	
navigation: ★ ★ ★ ★	
contents: ★ ★ ★	
readability: ★ ★ ★	
speed: ★ ★	
UK	

www.magicsponge.com
Magicsponge

Carling, the sponsors of Football's Premiership, have done their best to personalise this site for the fans of individual top flight clubs, which can be accessed via a drop-down menu in Switch Team at the top of the screen. Once you have made your choice, your club's name will appear in an appropriately coloured scarf and the background of the site will be in your colours. The other areas of the site can be accessed by clicking on the main menu, which runs across the screen just below Switch Team. Some of these sections though were still under construction at the time of writing.

The overall tone of the site is jokey and laddish, and some of the graphics look like they might belong in a Roy of the Rovers comic, but there is some useful information nevertheless.

SPECIAL FEATURES

Stats at a Glance gives a quick, graphic overview of your club's League position, Recent form for the last three matches, red and yellow cards, and the next fixture. The Recent form section is a little slow to update though.

Search this Site is a very useful interactive search tool, which allows you to narrow down your quest for information. If, for example, you type in the name of a player, then links are provided to an archive of all news articles within the site featuring that player.

Sidelines is the fan's chance to comment on recent performances. The views expressed tend to be thoughtful and of quite good quality. Have Your Say provides the opportunity to vote on a topical item, such as the goal of the season so far.

Saints and Grievances may be a fairly hopeless pun, but it does pick out the three best and worst aspects of your team's week. There is also a chance to vote for Your Carling Player of the Month.

Competition Time is a very simple trivia quiz and Trump It is a humorous look at various celebrities, although the rules are not easily comprehensible.

Club Results, Squad, Fixtures, Info and **History** all have their own link as does **Merchandise**, which provides a link to online retailer www.Kitbag.com.

Football Zone is devoted to more news articles, which again can be searched interactively. Abbreviated club sections can be accessed via the coloured links on the left of the screen.

Club Carling requires free registration to receive a magazine covering music, films and gadgets and competitions as well as football. The tone is unreconstructed lads and lager.

World Cup 2002 has some basic news on the competition so far. Neither the Game Zone or the Euro Zone were up and running at the time of writing.

The design of this site has a comic book quality and the tone is self-consciously laddish, but there is some good club info lurking below the surface.

sport

overall rating: ★ ★ ★ ★	
classification: news, video, comment, stats	
updated: frequently	
navigation: ★ ★ ★ ★	
contents: ★ ★ ★ ★	
readability: ★ ★ ★	
speed: ★ ★ ★ ★	
UK	

www.scotprem.com
Scottish Premier League

This site is a very useful information resource for all Scottish football fans, with the added bonus of an opportunity to download video clips of every goal scored in the Scottish Premier League. You can also tune into live match commentary for each and every match, courtesy of BBC Radio Scotland – great services for Scottish exiles. The site design is a little busy and cluttered but it's easy enough to get the information you need. The main menu is on the left, news stories appear in the centre, and links to specific club sections are on the right.

SPECIAL FEATURES

Video Clips of Goals can be accessed by clicking on Goal Videos at the top of the screen, Last Week's Goals on the right, or Video Goals Archive in the Interactive section of the main menu. You will need RealPlayer, but this is free and easy to obtain. Just follow the links on the screen. A modem connection of a speed greater than 220kbps is necessary to watch a video clip without downloading and saving its file first. Most modems in the UK have a top speed of 56 kbps so you will probably have to download. This will take a few minutes for a video clip of only a few seconds, and the final images are small and a bit jerky, but it is all well worth the effort to catch up on your team's goals.

SPL also offers live scores and live commentary on every match, with match commentary from BBC Radio Scotland.

Club News can be found down the right hand side of the screen and has links to sections for all of the SPL clubs. There you will find the latest news stories relating to your club and a section claiming to be Player Stats And Profiles, which at the time of writing proved to be just a list of players names and numbers.

MyScotPrem in the News section of the main menu lets you tailor the news you receive to your areas of interest. Once you have made your choice of SPL Individual Team News and General News Feeds, then these are the stories which will appear first on your SPL homepage.

News Archive is also in the News section, and allows you to search by year in an archive stretching back to 1997.

Official Links to the SPL Club websites are arranged neatly across the very top of the page.

OTHER FEATURES

All the tables, results and fixtures can be found in Statistics. Interactive provides an opportunity for you to vote for your Manager of the Month or download Screensavers and Wallpaper. Interactive also has a rather under-used Chat Forum. The main menu also has sections on the Under 21 League and the Youth competitions in the SPL. Broadcast has TV listings for live SPL games.

Video clips of every goal and live commentary for every match are a fantastic resource for soccer-starved Scottish exiles.

news sites

overall rating:	★ ★ ★ ★ ★
classification:	news, comment, scores
updated:	frequently
navigation:	★ ★ ★ ★ ★
contents:	★ ★ ★ ★ ★
readability:	★ ★ ★ ★
speed:	★ ★ ★ ★ ★
UK	

www.football365.com
The 365 Network

Football 365 is one of the most comprehensive internet football news, comment and statistics services around, and will have something of appeal for every football fan.

Football 365's strength is the sheer volume of material incorporated within the site. Clicking on any of the main menu items on the left of the screen reveals a dizzying amount of detail, but to the designers' credit, it is relatively easy to find what you want quickly.

The only criticism is that the content is not always quite as funny as the editor and journalists might like to think. Some of the humour is slightly flat.

The site has a smart, business-like appearance with the main menu sitting neatly down the left-hand side of the screen. If, however, you are a little short of time, then it is worth exploring the Essentials box on the right. This has a quick overview of the most important items of the days news, as well as a results round-up service.

SPECIAL FEATURES

Latest News & Reports brings you football news in just about every way imaginable. So you can indulge in Breaking News, Main News, News Flash, Latest Match Previews, Match Reports or Post-Match Press Conferences. Or if you are after something more specific, news is also broken down by Division and Competition, not to mention the Scottish section. Finally, if you are not too exhausted reading about it, you can send in your own match report via a DIY Match Report form.

Football 365 also offers the opportunity to receive their news packages by email, downloaded directly to your computer. This is best accessed in the Services section, which provides simple instructions on how to receive the full Football 365 Newspaper service or the briefer Essentials version. If you only want news from a particular club, then this is available too in the Choose Your Club section. Here you can visit a Homeground and sign up for the Club 365 email service.

Transfer Gossip is just that: a round-up of the rumour mills from the Premiership and beyond.

Audio & Video offers the opportunity to listen to the news via their own Radio F365 or via three daily Latest Audio Bulletins. This section has humorous video clips too, although some of these are a lot less humorous than others. It is necessary to download a free copy of RealPlayer before listening or watching.

Statistics is described as 'The Ultimate Anorak Guide' and for once it is worth believing the hype. Here you can access an absolute mass of stats from basic league tables to complex graphical representations of which teams are most likely to score when, goals per game, run of form, and even a team's resolve after falling behind in a match. All of this can be accessed by team, league or country. Finally, there is an interactive section, where you can judge a club's performance against various criteria, or see how they have fared over the years against particular opposition.

Fun & Games contains Carlsberg Mediawatch, and is a very useful catch-up service for all the football opinion, comment and rumour from the previous day's newspapers.

Live Matches provides a results and score in play service, as well as half-time reports, full-time reports, and text commentary on big matches.

England & Internationals is devoted to the international scene with news, opinion, results and tables for England, Scotland, Wales, Northern Ireland and the Republic of Ireland.

Features & Columns has an unusual mix of contributors, all of whom can be relied upon to provide a strong opinion. Here you can read weekly offerings from Sky pundit Andy Gray, broadcaster and founder of 365 Danny Kelly, and former broadcaster turned mystic David Icke. There are also a variety of special features and player interviews.

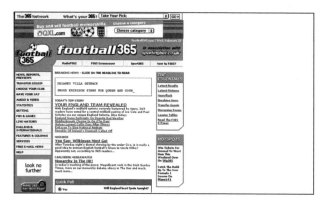

OTHER FEATURES

Have Your Say provides an opportunity for you to get things off your chest either by sending emails, joining a Discussion Forum, or filing your own Match Report. You can also have your Footy Questions answered or enter numerous Polls.

Fun & Games has plenty of sections to while away a wet afternoon. Here you can play Trivia Game, laugh at the Lookalikes, Picture Gags and Colemanballs, or send in a witty entry to the Caption Competition.

A dizzyingly comprehensive football news, comment and stats service, which leaves very few aspects of the game uncovered.

sport

overall rating: ★ ★ ★ ★ ★	
classification: news, statistics	
updated: frequently	
navigation: ★ ★ ★ ★ ★	
contents: ★ ★ ★ ★ ★	
readability: ★ ★ ★ ★ ★	
speed: ★ ★ ★ ★	
UK	

www.planetfootball.com
Planet Football

Planet Football is an excellent resource for any news-hungry football fan, and has the added attraction of being the online provider for the increasingly famous Opta Stats. The news service is well organised but it is with the Stats that Planet Football really makes its mark. They are thoughtfully presented and can be relied on to add a new dimension to pub arguments about which team has the best defence, or who is the best midfielder in the English or Scottish Premierships.

The website has a pleasing design with lots of photos to accompany the news stories. It is also easy to navigate. There are two main sections: the news menu on the left of the screen and the Opta menu on the right.

SPECIAL FEATURES

Planet Football offers a results and goals in play service in Matchday Scores and Breaking News, which can be found in the top right-hand corner of the screen.

The main menu, which runs down the left of the screen is mainly devoted to news service. This can be taken completely raw via Newsfeed, or packaged up into particular areas of interest, which cover just about every football angle for both the English fan and beyond. So you can home in on news from the English domestic competitions, European competitions, European domestic leagues, Las Americas, Global or International.

The **Club Index** has pages for every English league club and the Scottish Premier League clubs. Clicking on a club page will reveal a news section plus a list of the players in that club's squad. Clicking on a player's name leads to the Opta Stats (see below) for that player. These include this season's stats for an English or Scottish Premiership player but are limited to last season for players from lower leagues.

Planet Football's main claim to fame is the Opta Stats, which have their own panel and menu in the middle right of the screen.

Opta Stats are made up of an incredibly painstaking statistical analysis of football matches, which reduce teams and players to a series of numbers. This is a great tool for making statistical comparisons and, whether you find them fascinating or mind-numbingly boring, you cannot help but admire the work that has gone into compiling them.

In short, all the action in every English and Scottish Premiership match is analysed for goals, shots on and off target, passes completed, successful crosses, fouls made etc. This information is then used to rank each team and each player with an Opta Stat number.

Index lets you can see which are the best teams at skills such as tackling and shooting. Or you can see which are the highest ranked players by their playing position. Referees are also subjected to the Opta treatment to see who is most likely to give fouls or to brandish red and yellow cards. Finally, each week,

sport

Opta produce their Team of the Week, based on Opta scores and backed up with some humorous comments for each player.

Also in the Opta section is Opta Scout, which has interesting weekly in-depth reports on up-and-coming young players from both Britain and Europe.

Opta Jury is a weekly look at whether a recent transfer has been a success or failure by comparing a player's performance at the new and old clubs. And in Opta Classic, a great historical match such as the 1966 World Cup final is given the Opta Stats once-over. In Ask Tappers, you can get your player or team performance questions answered by emailing them in via an online form.

Previews compares statistics of opposing players before they have played the match and Results shows how they actually did, with the added bonus of a match report thrown in.

The funniest and most bizarre comments from the football world can be found in Quotes of the Week.

OTHER FEATURES

Planet Football has a Roy of the Rovers comic strip for the nostalgic fan and a mystery person quiz called Who Am I? for the trivia enthusiast.

Opta is where you can join a Fantasy Football league or play Tip'Em, a results prediction game. Or you can while away a few minutes completing the weekly football Crossword.

Listings for TalkRadio can be found in On Air and you can send your comments in to the radio station via email.

You can relive old times and catch up on all of those Opta Stats in Euro 2000 Review. And finally, the whole Opta process is explained in About Opta.

An efficient news service and absolutely thousands of those Opta Stats.

sport

overall rating:	★ ★ ★ ★ ★
classification:	news, comment
updated:	frequently
navigation:	★ ★ ★ ★ ★
contents:	★ ★ ★ ★
readability:	★ ★ ★ ★ ★
speed:	★ ★ ★ ★ ★

UK

www.teamtalk.com
Teamtalk

This is perhaps the most solid and authoritative football news service in what is a crowded sector of the market. The news stories are particularly well edited and presented and do not fall into the trap of trying to offer too much information just because that information is available. This would definitely be a good first stop off for news about your club.

The site is simply designed and easy to navigate with every section accessible from the main menu on the left. The typeface used in the articles themselves is slightly larger than normal and makes for a soothing read.

SPECIAL FEATURES

Top Stories has breaking news arranged by headline with an Archive link for previous days' stories. Fixtures can be searched interactively by entering a date of your choice. Your Say is used frequently by fans to make some well-informed comments. And in Audio, you can listen to the news rather than reading it. You will, however, need to download a free copy of RealPlayer before you can use this service.

Club News contains a link and a headline for every club in the English and Scottish Leagues, as well as a home nation National section. Each club's page has News, a news Archive, Stats, Fixtures, Club contact details and history, a Player section, and the chance to listen to specific club news in Audio Summary. The news sections are particularly strong with some solid reporting. The Player pages have some interesting biographical information, as well as some insightful pen portraits.

Peter Jackson Uncensored can be found within the Club News section and contains some informative thoughts on life in football's lower leagues. Peter Jackson had a long playing career and experience of management with Huddersfield Town FC.

FA Cup Diary uses a formula popularised by the BBC's Match of the Day in following a club right from the preliminary rounds of the FA Cup all the way to Wembley, or in this case all the way to Cardiff while Wembley is being rebuilt. If the original club is knocked out (inevitable at some point) then attention is turned to the victors and so on. There were some funny match reports and great photos from the very earliest rounds of 2000/01 at the time of writing.

Soccer DB is an interactive tool which allows you to view historical league tables and query the results record between individual teams since 1993/4. There is also an opportunity to buy this software, which can be used to attempt to predict the results of matches.

Local Heroes is a humorous column devoted to the highs, lows, trials and tribulations of Castle, a struggling club in the Burton and District Saturday League.

Sports Radio is a live radio station broadcasting from 1.30 to 5.30pm every Saturday afternoon. Again you will need

RealPlayer to tune in to a mixture of sports previews, interviews and results, which cover many sports beyond football.

Betting has a column from Boycie the Bookie, a spokesman with none other than the mighty Ladbrokes. Needless to say his tips are ambiguous to say the least. More direct betting ideas can be found in Our Advice, which has a useful table to show whether you would have won or lost in the long term by following the various tipsters' selections. There is also link direct to the Ladbrokes online site if you are feeling lucky.

OTHER FEATURES

Teamtalk has the usual selection of League Tables and a goals and results service in Match Day. Soapbox promises an opportunity for you to air your views on football topics but was not up and running at the time of writing.

World provides a link to www.teamtalkworld.com, which provides the same service as Teamtalk UK for selected big European and USA football clubs. Rugby leads to Teamtalk's equally authoritative oval ball service. There are various links to online retailers in Sports Books and Sports Stores.

Solid, reliable and with just the right amount of detail, this site is a model of clarity.

www.footballunlimited.co.uk
The Guardian and Observer Newspapers

This is a sophisticated online football newspaper from the publishers of The Guardian and the Observer. Most of the editorial and match reports can be read first in those newspapers, but there are dedicated online sections such as The Fiver, a daily email service.

The site is crisply designed and easy to navigate, with a main menu running across the screen just below the titles. It should appeal to any football fan who wants a little more from a site than just results and stats.

SPECIAL FEATURES

Fiver is a free daily email service of news, fixtures and TV listings. It is written especially for Football Unlimited and takes a wry, light hearted look at the day's football events. It is called The Fiver because it is mailed to your desktop every weekday at 5 pm. You will need to register for free before you can receive this service.

Breaking News contains all of the latest stories. Transfer speculation can be found in Rumours Unlimited in the homepage. Knowledge Unlimited is also on the homepage and contains the answers to football questions emailed to Football Unlimited. You can have your own questions answered by sending them to the boss@guardian.co.uk.

overall rating:	★ ★ ★ ★
classification:	news, comments, stats
updated:	frequently
navigation:	★ ★ ★ ★
contents:	★ ★ ★ ★ ★
readability:	★ ★ ★ ★ ★
speed:	★ ★ ★ ★
UK	

Clubs has a page for every club in the Premiership, First Division and Scottish Premier. These contain results, match reports, news items and squad details.

Columnists has an impressive array of football writers ranging from David Lacey to Ron Atkinson. Their articles, though, are first published in print in The Guardian or The Observer.

Special Reports takes you beyond the domestic game and has sections on the Champions League, the Uefa Cup, Continental Football, Euro 2000, the World Club Championship and the African Nations Cup. There is an also an area for past triumphs and failures in the FA Cup.

Games contains a vitriolic betting column from professional gambler Patrick Murray, a daily trivia Quiz, the glorious Ormondroyd's Virtual Match Reports (see page 96), an animated game called the Flying Ginolas, and articles from the magazine When Saturday Comes.

OTHER FEATURES

All the most recent statistical information can be found in Fixtures, Latest Scores, Tables and Statistics. You will need to register before airing your views in the chat forum All Talk. And you can search all football articles in Football Unlimited since September 1998 by typing in a key word.

A crisp, sophisticated online footie newspaper from The Guardian and The Observer.

www.soccerbase.com
The Mirror Group

The Soccerbase originated as a means of compiling betting information for Mirror Group newspapers. It contains a huge amount of statistical information, and claims to have the result of every English and Scottish league and cup match ever played. The site will appeal to any football fan who needs quick and reliable stats. Navigation is quite simple, although the mass of links means that there are many routes to the same place.

SPECIAL FEATURES

Latest has the week's results, scorers, red and yellow cards, transfers and management changes. Results, fixtures and tables can be found in Teams, along with squad stats.

Competitions has English, Scottish, European and International tables. Head to Head is an interactive tool, which allows you to access all time records between clubs. Transfers contains the latest activity by date, and is also searchable by team or by amount paid.

Managers has career details for current and past managers, and referees has a list of games officiated and cards given.

Season provides the winners of major football competitions for every year since 1871/2. Betting has fixed odds, spread betting and pools statistics for upcoming games.

Stats, stats and more stats presented clearly and effectively.

overall rating:	★ ★ ★ ★
classification:	statistics
updated:	every 15 minutes
navigation:	★ ★ ★ ★
contents:	★ ★ ★ ★ ★
readability:	★ ★ ★ ★
speed:	★ ★ ★ ★
UK	

sport

overall rating: ★ ★ ★ ★	
classification: online magazine	
updated: regularly	
navigation: ★ ★ ★ ★ ★	
contents: ★ ★ ★	
readability: ★ ★ ★	
speed: ★ ★ ★ ★	
UK	

www.extraordinaryworld.com
Extraordinary World

This is a compact, neatly designed website, which sets out to provide 'Football Fun for Football Fans'. The articles are well written and there are enough inventive items scattered throughout the site to make for a pleasant diversion.

Navigation is extremely simple with all sections accessed through the main menu at the top of the screen.

SPECIAL FEATURES

Magazine is divided into two sections. Shorts has some entertaining items such as the Most Annoying XI in the Premiership, a history of Ferocious Derbies and Match Day tales from those unsung heroes who actually work at football grounds on Saturday afternoons. Articles takes a more leisurely look at topical issues, including a section on Fanatical Fans and, at the time of writing, a campaign to drive the much maligned David Mellor out of football.

Famous Fans has in-depth interviews with illustrious football supporters. Fun and Games contains more weird and wonderful diversions for the fan with a few minutes to spare. Here you can learn how to dye your hair to resemble a football or click on links to the wackier regions of the football fan's world. Snap Shots invites you to send in a photo of yourself in an unusual footie fan situation plus a story about how you happened to be there.

Fan's League is a fast and furious trivia game that you play against an online opponent (if there is one available) to score points for your favourite club and move them up the league table. Win Now! in the top right-hand corner of the homepage just requires free registration to receive weekly Fan Mail and be entered into prize draws for signed kit, books, CDs, cash and beer.

OTHER FEATURES

Rant Forums provides four areas for you to share your thoughts on football and other matters. Football Pubs has links to two online pub review specialists. Face Value is an items for sale and items wanted section, although at the time of writing the ad with the most replies was for the man who wanted a girlfriend. There is a chance to buy the Extraordinary World book, T-Shirts and Postcards in The Shop. Useful Stuff was still under construction at the time of writing but promises to provide links to the best Football Fan Web Sites for all of the English Football League Clubs.

An entertaining, professionally produced site with its heart firmly in the right place.

sport

overall rating: ★ ★ ★ ★
classification: online magazine
updated: daily
navigation: ★ ★ ★ ★
contents: ★ ★ ★ ★
readability: ★ ★ ★
speed: ★ ★ ★ ★
UK

www.soccernet.com
ESPN

ESPN's slick, commercial football website, feels more like a newspaper than most football sites. The emphasis here is on opinion and comment rather than masses of stats, and there are plenty of named journalists writing jaunty articles.

Navigation is relatively simple with a straightforward main menu on the left of the page. The pages though have lots have small sub-divisions and can feel a little cluttered. The Homepage carries the current top news story and is packed with other articles from its in-house journalists. The Features and Columnists sections both explore the big issues of the day in a lively style.

SPECIAL FEATURES

Betting Tips are provided by the charmingly inept Percy. Stats has transfer details, leading scorer tables, a fair play league and a list of suspended players.

England has News, which can be accessed by League or Club. In Clubs, you will find results, fixtures, stories, features and usefully detailed player profiles. Players can also be accessed alphabetically via the Who's Who section. England's fortunes are similarly covered in National Team.

Scotland is presented along the same lines, although there are no player profiles or Who's Who area.

There is an interactive search option if you want to narrow a subject down or find out what has been happening to a particular player.

OTHER FEATURES

Football news from around the world is rounded up by Europe, Champs League, Global and World Cup 2002. There is also a Message Board.

A slick football newspaper with lots of opinions.

sport

overall rating: ★★★★	
classification: news, comments, stats	
updated: frequently	
navigation:	
contents:	
readability: ★★★	
speed: ★★★★	
UK	

www.thesun.co.uk/sport
News International

The online version of The Sun newspaper's soccer coverage has some useful information and comment for any football fan. The style is just as punchy and raunchy as its print counterpart. The site's design is bold, brassy and tabloid right down to its very own 'Red Top'. Navigation is easy with a straightforward main menu down the left of the screen.

SPECIAL FEATURES

Domestic contains a database searchable by English and Scottish league club, which contains news, statistics, match reports and match previews. There is also information on transfers, bookings and goal scorers, as well as squad details. The Irish and League of Wales sections have fixtures and tables only. For a filtered selection of news stories you can type your club's name into the News Wire box in the top left of the screen.

Talking Heads has comment and columns from such celebrities as Chelsea's Dennis Wise and former England striker and pundit Jimmy Greaves.

OTHER FEATURES

Football punting tips from Justin Palmer can be found in Betting and Fun n' Games has quizzes, a comic strip, nostalgia items and competitions for prizes.

More fixtures, results and tables can be found in International, Europe, Non League and Park. Live Action contains a results ticker, match previews, fixtures and results. Shopping has links to online retailers for football and non-football items.

A bold, punchy offering from The Sun.

sport

overall rating: ★ ★ ★ ★	
classification: news, scores, stats	
updated: frequently	
navigation: ★ ★ ★	
contents: ★ ★ ★ ★	
readability: ★ ★ ★	
speed: ★ ★ ★ ★	
UK	

www.footballnews.co.uk
The Football News Organisation Limited

This is an enthusiastic and ambitious site, which aims to carry more football stats and information than any other. It should, in time, appeal to any football fan from the Premiership supporter to the Sunday League player. The site is strong on picking up information from obscure leagues, and also has a very large photo gallery of professional action. Some of the photos are added impressively quickly after the matches are finished.

The design is reasonably stylish, although the use of lower case letters in the menus feels a bit dated, and the standard of spelling is unprofessionally poor. The site is reasonably easy to navigate once you're used to it. The main menu lies across the top of the screen and clicking on a category there will open a secondary menu which runs down the left of the screen.

SPECIAL FEATURES

News has the usual mix of breaking stories and match reports. Matches contains results, a form guide, charts and head-to-head team analysis to help in football betting.

Betting has a section called Luca's Tips (he wins apparently) and Luca's Column in which he explains his selections. There is also a mass of statistical information to help you predict the results of matches for both spread betting and fixed odds purposes.

Major Leagues Each of the major leagues in England has its own section containing a well-stocked photo gallery, news, fixtures and results, tables, and form guides. Clicking on a club name leads to more stats and a squad section.

Domestic and European Comps A similar amount of information can be found for the other major domestic and European competitions. The Europe section, though, tends to promise more than it can deliver, with a results-only service provided for some of the leagues.

Non-League is an ambitious attempt to gain information on all of the feeder leagues in England and Wales, and they already have results and team information from an impressively wide range of leagues. There are also sections on Welsh football and the Womens' game.

Referees has red and yellow card stats for all of the English and Scottish League referees.

OTHER FEATURES

Interactive has three chat forums called Football, Betting and Match Chat, although the latter was still under development at the time of writing. Fun has cartoons with audio but Shopping was yet to be launched at the time of review. There are a selection of polls to enter in Votes & Features and a live score ticker in Match Ticker #1 for live scores.

It is often a case of quantity over quality in this site, although the quantity is impressive in its own right.

overall rating: ★★★★	
classification: news, comment	
updated: frequently	
navigation: ★★★★	
contents: ★★★★	
readability: ★★★	
speed: ★★★	
UK	

www.zoofootball.com
Zoo Media Corporation

Zoo Football has a bubbly, irreverent editorial style and certainly could not be accused of taking its subject too seriously. The columnists are also an eccentric bunch with some unusual opinions so this site is not for the football fan who wants in-depth analysis and piles of stats. It is all very good natured though and has a speciality in its football betting and tipping service.

The screen design is a little busy and tends to go in for too many flashy, pointless graphics. It is, however, easy to navigate with a clear main menu on the left of the screen and links to other Zoo sites running across the top.

SPECIAL FEATURES

Today's News has both breaking stories and recent archive material arranged by Domestic competitions and Worldwide leagues and Cups. Paper View keeps a close eye on the tittle tattle from the British tabloids, while even more unlikely stories are covered in Rumour Mill. Transfer List has a useful series of tables showing all the transfer movements in the Premiership this season.

Zoobet's star writers can be reached either through Opinion in the main menu or further down in Columnists. Former England player and Republic of Ireland manager Jack Charlton can be relied on for strongly made, forthright opinions. Stan Bowles muses in flamboyant style and Alan Kennedy concentrates on Liverpool, his former club. Clearly though, Zoo Football regard their top writer to be Derek McGovern, a sports betting journalist who is ever eager to provide a tip or two.

Backchat provides an opportunity to email Zoo Football with an opinion on a footballing matter, the best of which are published and might also win you a T-shirt.

Features contains a mass of different ways of taking a sideways look at football, from tales of conflict past and present in Dribbling Rivalries, to football essays from far-flung places in Postcards from the Edge. There are also a series of good, well-written interviews with the very top names in the game and more serious articles, such as access to football grounds for disabled supporters, in Phil Investigates. Greatest Hits has another selection of humorous items.

Betting provides a link to www.Zoobet.com, a goldmine of betting tips and systems, as well as a guide to which online bookies are offering incentives when you open an account.

OTHER FEATURES

Future and past action is rounded up in Match Reports and Match Previews. You can have your own say in Message Board and Chat Room, although the fainthearted may be put off by the warnings of the possibility of strong language.

Links to the other sites in the Zoo Network can be found in the menu which runs across the top of the page. There are big cash prizes to be won in ZooFantasy2001, a football fantasy game. There are more chat forums in Zoofc, Zoofootballchat and Zoochat. Kidzunited is for pre and young teen football fans and contains cartoons, games and competitions. Zooticker allows you to receive a 'live' newsfeed and goals service, and Zootropolis is an online shop, selling everything from clothes to books and videos.

A bubbly site with some outspoken columnists and lots of betting tips.

www.scottishfootball.com
Scotland On Line

This is a useful stats and comment resource for the Scottish football fan. However, it is not the easiest site to navigate and the design feels a little dated.

SPECIAL FEATURES

News has top stories, a searchable archive, match reports and analysis. News can also be filtered by league division.

The Hot Seat is a weekly column featuring manager interviews and is accessible via the panel on the homepage. Richard Gordon, the respected journalist, also has a weekly column – reached via the homepage or Features in the main menu.

Newsletter is a free weekly email service containing reports, previews and transfer gossip. The club section can be found in a green panel on the middle right of the homepage. Here you can filter news and stats for your favourite club.

OTHER FEATURES

All of the usual stats can be found in Live Scores, League Tables and Leading Scorers. Fitba Facts is a trivia service, and there are Comic Strips, Competitions and a Card Gallery of Scottish heroes.

Useful but rather old-fashioned feeling Scottish football service.

overall rating:	
classification: news, comments, stats	
updated: frequently	
navigation:	
contents:	
readability:	
speed:	
UK	

sport

miscellaneous

overall rating: ★ ★ ★ ★
classification: news, information
updated: regularly
navigation: ★ ★ ★ ★ ★
contents: ★ ★ ★ ★
readability: ★ ★ ★ ★
speed: ★ ★ ★ ★
UK

www.leaguemanagers.com
League Managers Association

This is a little jewel of a website, which will appeal to every English football fan. It is neatly designed, easily navigated, refreshingly unpretentious, and contains some fascinating biographical information on football managers. It also provides a shop window for those managers currently out of work.

SPECIAL FEATURES

Latest News has a well-edited selection of stories, covering news items that directly affect football managers. It also has recorded interviews with managers, although you will need to download a free copy of RealAudio to listen to them.

Members allows you to catch up on the CVs of the managers in the LMA. For each manager, there is a photo, a list of clubs managed and a short biography. But perhaps the most interesting reading is the list of available managers, the poor souls (many of them illustrious) who are currently without a club.

Anorak Stats has a bitesize selection of topical statistical oddities. Stats is a longevity league for football managers. At the time of writing, Dario Gradi of Crewe Alexandra was the longest serving, having avoided the sack since June 1983.

OTHER FEATURES

LMA History explains the origins and aims of the LMA, which was founded on the initiative of Graham Taylor, the former England manager. In Awards, you can find details of the Manager of the Month awards run by the LMA.

A tightly focused website, which has lots of useful information about professional football managers.

sport

overall rating:	★ ★ ★
classification:	information
updated:	regularly
navigation:	★ ★ ★ ★
contents:	★ ★ ★
readability:	★ ★ ★
speed:	★ ★
UK	

www.wembleynationalstadium.co.uk
Wembley National Stadium

This website will appeal to anybody who has ever been to Wembley Stadium or is simply curious about what the new stadium will look like. Navigation is easy in what is a simple site, although the design is self-consciously 'hi-tech' in the Stadium section and 'heritage' in the End of an Era section.

SPECIAL FEATURES

Stadium has details of the Design and Timetable for construction of the new Wembley. Stadium Comparisons shows how the new stadium will shape up against other major stadia in Europe. Image Gallery has artists' impressions of both inside and outside the new arena, although these were very slow to download.

Webcam gives you the dubious pleasure of being able to watch the Twin Towers being demolished and the new stadium rise in their place. Images are updated every five minutes.

End of an Era in the top right corner of the screen takes you to www.wembley-endofanera.com, where you can delve into the history of the Old Wembley, once described by Pele as the 'Church of Football'. There is also the opportunity here to visit the Memorabilia Shop, where you can buy mementoes from the old stadium, including sections of turf and match programmes.

A good site for a quick visit to see how the new Wembley is progressing.

enthusiasts' sites

www.non-league.net
Non-League on the Net (NLOTN)

This site is an absolutely fantastic resource for the non-league football fan. Each of the major leagues is covered in great depth but there is no excuse if you feel that your league or team is under represented – it is up to the supporter to provide the information to keep the website going.

The design is clear, well thought-out and easy to navigate, with a main menu on the left of the screen. Photographs are well used to illustrate the news stories and add to the professional feel of the site, although the pages are much quicker to download if you select 'text only' on the home page.

SPECIAL FEATURES

News relies heavily on information provided by the non-league supporter on the ground, but the correspondents who compile the previews, comment and match reports are professional journalists. A different writer is responsible for Conference, Dr Marten's, Unibond, Scottish and Other Non-League Football respectively. The standard of reporting is uniformly solid and highly informative. There is an Archive news section if you need to catch up on some past facts.

overall rating:	★ ★ ★ ★ ★
classification:	news, stats, comment
updated:	regularly
navigation:	★ ★ ★ ★ ★
contents:	★ ★ ★ ★
readability:	★ ★ ★ ★ ★
speed:	★ ★ ★ ★
UK	

Reports is a section written wholly by the non-league supporter and would-be match reporter. NLOTN aim to publish two fan's match reports per week, so it is well worth taking along your notebook and pen if you are at a top match. NLOTN also provide some writing guidelines to ease your passage into web print.

Results is an absolutely massive database of all the League results and tables for the first nine levels of football in England. In practice this means you can find a result from the Carling Premiership to the Dorset Combination including every league in between. This service is provided via a link called, rather prosaically, The English Football Pyramid and Cup Competitions. This takes you to www.footballpyramid.co.uk, which is in itself a minor miracle of organisation and colour coding to show how the pyramid of football leagues is constructed.

The **Links** section is a similarly vast resource with hundreds of well-organised links to official and unofficial non-league football club websites.

Fanzines has some dispassionate reviews of the fanzines of non-league clubs plus links if available.

OTHER FEATURES

Features has Season Reviews for last season and League Previews for the forthcoming action, and Forums carries links to the message and chat sections of non-league clubs' websites.

A top notch site for the non-league football fan. Masses of well-written and enthusiastically presented information.

www.footie51.co.uk
Footie51 Football Matters – online football magazine

Footie51 is a professionally produced football fanzine, which will appeal to any football fan who wants more than breaking news, transfer gossip and results. The site is easy on the eye, with good graphics and easy-to-read white type on a black background. However, it isn't easy to navigate. Clicking on the main index in the centre of the screen leads to other non-specific areas of the homepage, which can be frustrating. It is worth persevering with clicking on any of the links around the homepage, though, which generally lead to excellent content.

SPECIAL FEATURES

Interview has some thought provoking discussions with writers and journalists about their views on the game.

Articles, on the other hand, are written by fans, many of whom could be journalists judging by the quality of their writing.

Book Review lets you catch up on the best of the crowded football book market and recommends the current top buys.

Footie on Film has a comprehensive list plus reviews of virtually every film, good or bad, ever made with a football theme.

Shirt is a very sharp comic strip about the fate and fortunes of Swindleton United.

overall rating:	★ ★ ★ ★
classification:	fanzine
updated:	monthly
navigation:	★ ★ ★
contents:	★ ★
readability:	★ ★ ★ ★ ★
speed:	★ ★ ★ ★
UK	

Formations has some inventive and witty graphics depicting the foibles of players and teams.

Not the News is a tongue-in-cheek look at the more bizarre recent football events.

At the Bar is an amusing spoof diary of a less than brilliant football team, who tend to be more interested in post match lubrication than in the match itself.

Footie51 also provides an excellent set of well-maintained links to other like-minded sites:

Nostalgia leads to good quality websites devoted to yesterday's top teams, like the Leeds United team of the Sixties and Seventies and the Holland team of 1974.

Homage details sites lovingly devoted to the great players such as Pele and George Best.

Fanzines has a very comprehensive listing of top quality football fanzines with links where available.

OTHER FEATURES

Competitions provides the opportunity to win books, videos and beer; sadly, the competitions were closed at the time of writing. Perhaps unwisely for a periodical, there is also Footie 51's Fixture Guide, which was also out of date at the time of review.

A top quality, professionally produced, thoughtful fanzine. Great content.

www.ormondroyd.co.uk
Ormondroyd's Virtual Match Reports

overall rating:
★ ★ ★ ★

classification:
humour

updated:
periodically

navigation:
★ ★ ★ ★

contents:
★ ★ ★

readability:
★ ★ ★ ★ ★

speed:
★ ★

UK

This is one of the funniest football sites on the web and, although it is devoted to Fulham, any football fan will see their own experiences reflected in Ormondroyd's joys and frustrations. A series of stick cartoons make up a match report, as well as his journey to and from the ground. It might not sound that great, but he has a blindingly funny line in sarcastic humour too.

The site is very easy to navigate with a main menu below the main title. The match reports themselves can be a little slow to load but it is well worth the wait.

SPECIAL FEATURES

You can enter Ormondroyd's world by clicking on any of the underlined links in the main menu. Here Ormondroyd has produced reports from the 1998/1999 season to date Occasionally, Ordmondroyd spreads his wings into other media and you could read his reports for The Guardian newspaper in the Football Unlimited section.

The very latest reports and any special features can be found via the links to the right of the title.

Some of the best sports humour on the internet.

sport

overall rating: ★ ★ ★ ★	
classification: entertainment	
updated: regularly	
navigation: ★ ★ ★ ★	
contents: ★ ★ ★ ★	
readability: ★ ★ ★ ★	
speed: ★ ★ ★ ★	
UK	

www.predictionleague.co.uk
Three Ball Cascade Software

Prediction League is a simple but devilishly addictive interactive game, which allows you to pit your wits against pals and strangers in predicting the results of football matches. What is more, it is all completely free. The design of the site is strictly no frills and functional but don't let that put you off. Once you have predicted your first match and seen your name on the league table, you will be coming back every week.

SPECIAL FEATURES

To be able to play Prediction League, you need a player name and a password, and to get these you need to predict the result of a match. To find your team of choice, click on one of the football league buttons on the main menu on the left of the screen.

Now click on the link to your team and you will find a list of matches. Click on a match and fill in the boxes to make your prediction. You can click on Form, View, Squad or Latest News to help you make a more informed decision. Most points are earned for getting the result right, but there are bonuses for predicting scores and scorers accurately.

If all of this seems too simple, you can also play the Ultimate game, which involves predicting the result of every match in a division. Good luck!

A simple, fun, free, interactive game. Get predicting!

www.footballgroundguide.co.uk
The Internet Football Ground Guide by Duncan Adams

This is a brilliant resource for any away football fan who wants to know what to expect before travelling. Each Football League club is covered in meticulous detail and a selection of personal anecdotes lets you into the world of a fan who is passionate about his subject.

The design would not win any style awards but who cares when the content is this good? Navigation is straightforward.

SPECIAL FEATURES

The heart of the site lies below the main menu on the homepage. For each League club you will find contact information, links to official and unofficial websites and photos of the ground. There are also sections called What's The Ground Like and What's It Like For Visiting Supporters, which give a personal but admirably clear picture of what to expect on a first visit.

In addition, there are recommendations on where to eat and drink and transport links. You might also find a selection of further information, such as the ground layout, disabled facilities, admission prices and future stadium developments.

overall rating: ★ ★ ★	
classification: information	
updated: regularly	
navigation: ★ ★ ★ ★	
contents: ★ ★ ★ ★ ★	
readability: ★ ★ ★ ★ ★	
speed: ★ ★ ★	
UK	

OTHER FEATURES

The main menu has details about the 92 Club, although you will have to visit all 92 Football League clubs before you can join. Around a thousand people have apparently. There are also links to other sports stadium sites, a section on English non-league football grounds, a Wembley section, and a nostalgia area for old or demolished stadiums.

A fantastic resource and labour of love all rolled into one.

www.soccerupdate.com
Soccerupdate

This site is a model of getting information across in the simplest way possible, and will appeal to any Premiership fan who wants quick and efficient team and transfer news. There is also a very full transfer rumours section, which leaves no bit of hearsay untouched.

The design is uncluttered, although individual pages can be rather long, and navigation is very simple indeed.

SPECIAL FEATURES

The homepage carries an up-to-date League table, a section wishing Happy Birthday to the day's birthday boy players, recent fixtures and results, and a very brief news and transfers section.

Team News has fixtures, suspensions, injury news, latest news and details of the squad used for the last match. There is also a list of transfer listed players or those rumoured to be on the move.

Transfer News contains information on all Premiership transfers and loans since August 1998. The archive is searchable by month.

Gossip is a very long list of all the transfer rumours doing the rounds. The section contains a date, the player involved, where he may be moving from and to, and any additional comments.

overall rating:	★ ★ ★
classification:	stats, rumours
updated:	frequently
navigation:	★ ★ ★ ★
contents:	★ ★ ★ ★
readability:	★ ★ ★
speed:	★ ★ ★ ★ ★
DK	

OTHER FEATURES

Fixtures & Results has a long list of scores, scorers and attendances, while Links has details of other like-minded football sites.

An excellent way of getting last-minute Premiership stats and gossip.

English Football League Clubs - Official Sites 2000/1 Season

Carling Premiership
Arsenal www.arsenal.co.uk
Aston Villa www.astonvilla-fc.co.uk
Bradford City www.bradfordcity.co.uk
Charlton Athletic www.charlton-athletic.co.uk
Chelsea www.chelseafc.co.uk
Coventry City www.ccfc.co.uk
Derby County www.dcfc.co.uk
Everton www.evertonfc.com
Ipswich Town www.itfc.co.uk
Leeds United www.lufc.co.uk
Leicester City www.lcfc.co.uk
Liverpool www.liverpoolfc.net
Manchester City www.mcfc.co.uk
Manchester United www.manutd.com
Middlesborough www.mfc.co.uk
Newcastle United www.nufc.co.uk
Southampton www.saintsfc.co.uk
Sunderland www.sunderland-afc.com
Tottenham Hotspur www.spurs.co.uk
West Ham United www.whufc.co.uk

Nationwide League Division One
Barnsley www.barnsleyfc.co.uk
Birmingham City www.bcfc.com
Blackburn Rovers www.rovers.co.uk
Bolton Wanderers www.boltonwfc.co.uk
Burnley www.clarets.co.uk
Crewe Alexandra www.crewealex.net (under construction)

Crystal Palace www.cpfc.co.uk
Fulham www.fulham-fc.co.uk
Gillingham www.gillinghamfootballclub.com
Grimsby Town www.gtfc.co.uk
Huddersfield Town www.htafc.com
Norwich City www.canaries.co.uk
Preston North End www.pnefc.co.uk
Portsmouth www.portsmouthfc.co.uk
Queens Park Rangers www.qpr.co.uk
Sheffield United www.sufc.co.uk
Sheffield Wednesday www.swfc.co.uk
Stockport County www.webserv1.stockport mbc.gov.uk/scfc/
Tranmere Rovers www.tranmererovers.co.uk
Watford www.watfordfc.co.uk
West Bromwich Albion www.wba.co.uk
Wimbledon www.wimbledon-fc.co.uk
Wolverhampton Wanderers www.wolves.co.uk

Nationwide League Division Two
Bournemouth www.afcb.co.uk
Brentford www.brentfordfc.co.uk
Bristol City www.bcfc.co.uk
Bristol Rovers www.bristolrovers.co.uk
Bury www.buryfc.co.uk
Cambridge United none at present
Colchester www.cufc.co.uk
Luton Town www.lutontown.co.uk
Millwall www.millwallfc.co.uk
Northampton Town www.ntfc.co.uk
Notts County www.nottscountyfc.co.uk
Oldham Athletic www.oldhamathletic.co.uk
Oxford United www.oufc.co.uk

sport

Peterborough United www.theposh.com
Port Vale www.port-vale.co.uk
Reading www.readingfc.co.uk
Rotherham United www.themillers.co.uk/rufc/
Stoke City none at present
Swansea City www.swansfc.co.uk
Swindon Town www.swindonfc.co.uk
Walsall www.saddlers.co.uk
Wigan Athletic www.wiganlatics.co.uk
Wrexham www.wrexhamafc.co.uk
Wycombe Wanderers none at present

Nationwide League Division Three

Barnet none at present
Blackpool www.blackpoolfc.co.uk
Brighton and Hove Albion
www.seagulls.co.uk
Cardiff City www.cardiffcity.co.uk
Carlisle United www.carlisleunited.co.uk
Cheltenham Town www.cheltenhamtown.co.uk
Chesterfield www.spireites.com
Darlington www.darlingtonfc.net
Exeter City under construction
Halifax Town none at present
Hartlepool United www.hartlepoolunited.co.uk
Hull City www.hullcity.org.uk
Kidderminster Harriers www.harriers.co.uk
Leyton Orient www.leytonorient.com
Lincoln City www.redimps.com
Macclesfield Town www.mtfc.co.uk
Mansfield Town none at present
Plymouth Argyle www.pafc.co.uk
Rochdale www.rochdale-football-club.co.uk

Scunthorpe United www.scunthorpe-united.co.uk
Shrewsbury Town www.shrewsburytown.co.uk
Southend United www.southendunited.co.uk
Torquay United www.torquayunited.com
York City www.yorkcityfc.co.uk

Scottish Premier

Aberdeen www.afc.co.uk
Celtic www.celticfc.co.uk
Dundee www.dundeefc.co.uk
Dundee United www.dundeeunited.co.uk
Dunfermline Athletic www.pars.resourcez.com
Heart of Midlothian www.heartsfc.co.uk
Hibernian www.hibs.co.uk
Kilmarnock www.kilmarnockfc.co.uk
Motherwell www.motherwellfc.co.uk
Rangers www.rangers.co.uk
St Johnstone www.stjohnstonefc.co.uk
St Mirren www.stmirren.net

section 4

golf

official sites

overall rating: ★ ★ ★ ★ ★	
classification: news, stats, information	
updated: frequently	
navigation: ★ ★ ★ ★ ★	
contents: ★ ★ ★ ★ ★	
readability: ★ ★ ★ ★ ★	
speed: ★ ★ ★ ★	
UK	

www.europeantour.com
PGA European Tour

This is a superb resource for any golf fan, which covers every tee, fairway, green, bunker and player on the European Tour. If you want latest news and scores, or have a specific question on future or past events, this site is sure to answer your query. The design is crisp and clear, with the main menu at the top of the screen and sub-menus on the left. All of the sections are presented in an admirably simple way.

SPECIAL FEATURES

Live Real-time scores for the European, Seniors and Challenge Tours can be accessed in this section, which also has a scores archive for this year's and last year's events.

News contains previews, breaking stories and an archive, which is searchable by week or by keyword.

Players is an impressive database, best accessed via the Player Browser section. Typing in the name of a player leads to his biography, profile, photograph, career wins, and his scoring and earnings record for every round he has ever played on the tour. The latter items are searchable by year. And if your man is famous enough, there will also be a link to an image library of zoomable photographs which show him in action at various events.

Events contains a mass of information about each tournament. You can search by event or venue to get a preview of the competition details including the player entry list, prize money, and past winners. The year's Tour Schedules can also be found here, as well as a Schedule and an archive for the Ryder Cup.

Stats Each player on the European Tour is analysed according to AXA Performance Data, the results of which can be found here. This is the place for the lowdown on who is best for Driving Accuracy, Driving Distance, Greens in Regulation, Average Putts, Putts in GIR, Sand Saves and Stroke Average.

Rankings is another statistical feast. This section contains Orders of Merit for all three Tours, European Tour Career Earnings, World Rankings, and the leaders in the race for Europe and US Ryder Cup Qualification Points.

TV & Video allows you to view brief Video Highlights of the latest action, although you will need RealPlayer. TV schedules and the various broadcast times of the TV round-up package European Tour Weekly can also be found here.

OTHER FEATURES

Tour Extra has some useful advice from the experts in Pro Tips and the chance to buy discounted copies of the millennium edition of the European Tour Yearbook, as well as more detail about the PGA European Tour's administrative structure.

A crisply structured, clearly presented resource for every question ever asked about the European Tour.

sport

overall rating: ★ ★ ★ ★ ★
classification: news, scores, info, mag
updated: frequently
navigation: ★ ★ ★ ★
contents: ★ ★ ★ ★ ★
readability: ★ ★ ★ ★
speed: ★ ★ ★ ★ ★
US

www.pgatour.com with golfweb.com
PGA Tour and Golfweb magazine

This is a vast website, which covers just about every subject imaginable to do with US golf. The fusion of the PGA Tour site with the Golfweb magazine site has created a compelling mixture of news, scores, reports, features and playing tips, which will appeal to any golf fan.

Surprisingly for such professional content, the site lags behind a little in its design, which is functional rather than funky. It is reasonably easy to navigate, once you have established that the PGA element is in the menu at the top of the screen, and the Golfweb magazine element is in the menu on the left.

SPECIAL FEATURES

All the facts and figures for the PGA Tour can be found in the menu running across the top of the screen.

Scores contains Full Leaderboards for the PGA Tour, the Seniors PGA Tour and the Buy.com Tour, as well as links to scoreboards for other pro tours. Schedules is a similarly comprehensive diary of all the professional golf events going on around the world.

Players is searchable alphabetically and contains a photo, biographical details, personal info and money-earning records for each player. There is also a mind boggling array of statistics, ranging from driving distances to putts per round, scoring averages, birdie stats and hole performance. All the statistics produce individual rankings and are searchable for every year that a particular player has been on the tour.

Stats covers a lot of the above information but allows more direct comparison between players, as well as giving money-earning Rankings, World Golf Rankings and Scoring Rankings.

PGA Tour Shop is a vast emporium containing bags, balls, books, clubs, clothes, gifts, shoes and accessories. It is possible to order from the UK but you will need to buy a substantial amount of merchandise as the minimum shipping rate comes to a whopping US$45.

The site's magazine section is contained in the menu which runs down the left-hand side of the screen.

My Leaderboard allows you to customise a desktop leaderboard so that you can follow the progress of ten players of your choice.

Life On Tour is a mixed bag of feature articles, letters from readers, tales from the cut-throat world of the Qualifying School, pros' diaries, and a 'Where Are They Now?' section. You can learn more about the professional golfer's world in Chat with a Pro, which invites you to submit email questions for answers by a top star.

Audio & Video is where the magazine section really comes to life. You will need to download a copy of RealPlayer before watching daily Video Highlights, listening to online Radio, or visiting the Press Room to watch video clips of interviews with players. It is well worth the effort though, even if playing streaming videos on a 56kbps connection can be a little jerky.

A potted version of all that is best from this website can be delivered to your desktop every week via a Free Newsletter. You need to fill out a brief subscription form before receiving news, feature columns, stats, instruction tips and details of shopping deals and bargains.

The **Practice Tee** section has a mass of hints and tips on how the amateur can improve his game. Here you can find everything from the Rules of Golf to the latest Equipment, sports psychology in the Head Game and how to avoid injury in Fitness. There are also special sections on how to play difficult shots in Shape of Swing, and insights into the tricks of the tour in Pro Tips.

OTHER FEATURES

Golf course reviews and details of US golfing holidays can be found in Travel. There are competitions and online golf simulation games in Games. Video Highlights of The Players Championship can be viewed in Live @ 17. In Shopping, you can buy tickets for events or used equipment in Golf Club Trader, or view a huge selection of Classifieds, although this section is obviously aimed at US residents. Finally, there is a selection of well chosen links in Special Sites.

A huge and compelling resource for everything to do with the US golf scene.

www.opengolf.com
Official site for the Open golf championship

overall rating:
★ ★ ★ ★ ★

classification:
news, scores, virtual tours

updated:
frequently during Open

navigation:
★ ★ ★ ★

contents:
★ ★ ★ ★ ★

readability:
★ ★ ★ ★

speed:
★ ★ ★ ★

UK

This is another site which really comes into its own when live competition is in progress – the site recorded 128 million page impressions during the 2000 Open at St Andrews. It is, however, worth a visit at other times, if only to remind yourself of past action, learn about ticket information for the next Open, or go on a virtual tour of an Open course. While the Open was in progress, all the latest developments and news could be accessed in Today At St Andrews, or live, hole-by-hole scores followed in Leaderboard.

The site has a pleasantly up-to-date design and navigation is via a concise main menu on the right of the screen.

SPECIAL FEATURES

Course is a fun way of going on an interactive tour of the current or most recent Open course. You can first choose a hole from a course map and for the 2000 Open at St Andrews, 1999 winner Paul Lawrie describes how he would approach playing it. You can also go up in a virtual helicopter for a Fly By Video of the hole, but you will need a copy of RealPlayer or Windows Multimedia. Finally, you can make a Virtual Tour of each hole courtesy of Ipix, who provide a 360 degree view from Tee, Fairway and Green.

MediaWorld has a great collection of both video and still images from the latest Open. RealPlayer or Windows Multimedia is again required to view the videos. You can zoom in and out of the photographs, although this is a bit time consuming, or search the entire database by player's name or keyword.

Players contains a photo and the Open Championship Record for each of the current competitors.

History is a comprehensive section where you can catch up on 25 accounts of classic competition in Past Opens. View all the scores since 1970 in Past Results, see a complete list of Champions, study how the Prize Money has increased from the £6 awarded in 1864, or reflect on the Open Records.

OTHER FEATURES

During the championship, you can watch the action unfold from a series of strategically placed Webcams. Ticket and travel details are available in Information. The Shop, managed by The Golf Warehouse, is always open and stocks a selection of branded socks, shirts, sweaters and hats, which can be shipped anywhere in the world.

In the top right-hand corner of the screen there is a link to The R & A website. This is organisation that runs the Open and various amateur competitions, as well as administering the Rules of Golf. You can learn more about the R & A's work via this link or going direct to www.randa.org.

A well-constructed site that is an essential source of information while the Open is progress.

www.masters.org
US Masters

This is another site powered by IBM and shares a lot of similarities with the sites for the Grand Slam Tennis Championships. It is clearly at its best when the tournament is in progress but it also has a very impressive virtual tour of the famous old course if you can't wait for the action to start. The site has a solid, stately sort of style, which befits a tournament redolent with history and a certain sort of pomp. It is simplicity itself to navigate, with a clear main menu at the top of the screen. You will need a copy of RealPlayer to watch the video sections within the site.

SPECIAL FEATURES

Course is about as close as you can get to experiencing what it is like at Augusta without actually being there. A Walking Tour of the Course contains panoramic views of key points around the course, including a peek inside the Champions Locker Room. Enlarged View allows you to fly over a hole in a helicopter, as well as viewing a 3-D animation of all the contours, bunkers and water hazards at Augusta. Landmarks is a video tour of the course complete with clips of classic action at some of the more famous holes. To complete the section, you can read Jack Nicklaus's comments on each hole in History.

The other main sections are obviously at their best when the tournament is in progress.

overall rating:
★ ★ ★ ★

classification:
scores, news, virtual tours

updated:
frequently during Masters

navigation:
★ ★ ★ ★ ★

contents:
★ ★ ★ ★

readability:
★ ★ ★ ★

speed:
★ ★ ★ ★

US

Today at the Masters has photos in Images of the Day, a photographic archive, Headlines and a News archive. There are also Player Interviews with the day's star performers direct from the press room. These can be read in text form or viewed or video, although the latter requires a copy of RealPlayer. The Players contains brief biographies and details of how the player has performed in previous Masters tournaments. Interactive is a super tool, which allows you to view what is going on around the course via Course Cams or Remote Cams. The latter you can also operate with your mouse for the complete interactive experience.

OTHER FEATURES

You can keep up with all the scores as they happen during play in Leaderboard. And History is a good resource for learning how the tournament started, who has won it, and what the trophies look like. You can also order commemorative books online in the Library in the History section.

A slick scores and interviews site with a great virtual tour.

www.lpga.com
Ladies Professional Golf Association

This is a very valuable site for any fan of women's golf, and great for catching up with how the Europeans are faring on the US tour. It is not the easiest site to navigate, however, with three main menus containing many similar links at top, left and bottom of screen. The design with its small typeface is rather busy and tiring on the eye.

SPECIAL FEATURES

The Tour contains Headline news, tour Schedules and links to Individual Tour Sites. You can also find out about Ticket Information, The Majors, and qualifying tournaments.

Player Biographies contains details of every player on the tour. including career highlights, statistics for the previous year, and year-by-year records for the Majors and LPGA tournaments.

Improve Your Game contains a fun and educational Online Animated Instruction Area from www.mysportsguru.com

OTHER FEATURES

The LPGA's developmental work can be found in Youth Programs. There is a well-stocked pro shop and a history of the LPGA in Women.

A useful resource for any fan of ladies' golf.

overall rating:	★★★
classification:	news, scores, info
updated:	frequently
navigation:	★★
contents:	★★★★
readability:	★★★
speed:	★★★★
US	

sport

overall rating: ★ ★	
classification: news, scores, reports	
updated: regularly	
navigation: ★ ★ ★ ★	
contents: ★ ★ ★	
readability: ★ ★	
speed: ★ ★	
UK	

www.ladieseuropeantour.com
Ladies European Tour

The Ladies' European Tour is very much a poor relation of its sister, USA based LPGA Tour, which is reflected in this rather spartan website. If you are looking for basic information about Ladies' European golf, though, there should be enough here to satisfy you. The site design is plain, and suffers from a lack of photos, though is easy enough to navigate.

SPECIAL FEATURES

Home contains the latest news, scores and a Features section, in which a top player is profiled. News allows you to search back through the archive by date and headline.

Schedule and Results lists all the tour details, with additional card and scoring analysis in Leaderboard. Statistics is an interactive database, which you can search by Player, Tournament or Moneylist.

Solheim Cup contains all the results, scores, reports, history and player profiles for this bi-annual clash.

OTHER FEATURES

Players contains a photo and very brief career details of ten of the top European players. The Photo Gallery is similarly sparse with only eight photos of players in action.

Basic information on the Ladies' European Tour.

news sites

www.golfonline.com
Golf Magazine published in the US

If you subscribe to Golf Magazine, you might well have read most of the material in this site already. But if you are prepared to wait a month, then you can see it online for free here. The result is a formidable resource on all things golf, which will appeal to fan and player alike.

The style of the site is a little cutesy, with eighteen sections representing the eighteen holes of golf, which leads to some overlapping of content within sections. Navigation is very easy though. The eighteen sections are in a main menu on the left of the screen. Once you are in a section you can read the headline article in On The Tee or catch up on more detail in Through the Green.

SPECIAL FEATURES

Tours has all the latest information for the professional game, including schedules and statistics.

Instruction contains an amazing number of ways to improve your game. You can browse through the Tips of the Day, Brush up on the Basics, learn from golf Clinics, watch Animated Lessons, or Analyze Your Game in the Interactive Golf Academy, just for starters.

overall rating:
★ ★ ★ ★

classification:
news, instruction, comment

updated:
regularly

navigation:
★ ★ ★ ★

contents:
★ ★ ★ ★

readability:
★ ★ ★

speed:
★ ★ ★ ★

US

Equipment has recent technological advances, a Clubs Tested section, and a glimpse into what the pros put into their bag before trying to win another million dollars.

Courses/Travel is clearly of most use if you are planning a golfing trip to the US, although it does have listings and reviews for some UK and European courses. It also has the intriguingly named Golf Orgies section, which transpires to be holidays tailored for people who want to play non-stop golf from dawn 'til dusk.

News, columnists and feature articles are covered both in Golfweek and in News/Features. The latter, in particular, has some good, in depth interviews with pro golfers.

Senior Golfer has lots of articles from Senior Golfer print magazine. Women's Golf has all the latest from the LPGA Tour, equipment guides, tips and online tuition. Junior Golf has everything you need to know about getting your kids started.

OTHER FEATURES

Rules has all the answers to those tricky regulations and etiquette problems. Community has a selection of message and chat forums. You can work out and shape up in Fitness, read more reviews and columns in Opinions, or learn how to become a pro in Feedback. Finally, you can scour the site in Search or subscribe to the print version of Golf Magazine.

Opinions, tips, and golf articles galore.

www.golftoday.co.uk
Golf Today Online Magazine

The jury is still out on this ambitious but as yet fledgling UK online golf magazine. Golf Today carries an impressive number of sections but a lot of its content is still a little thin and it remains to be seen whether it will live up to expectations. There is, though, a reasonable amount to enjoy for both golf fan and player. The homepage has links to the live scoreboards of the major professional events going on around the world, as well as a selection of latest headline news articles.

Navigation appears simple enough at first glance with a main menu across the top of the screen. However, reaching a lot of the sections involves connecting to sister sites, which open another window making the process fiddly. The worthwhile Amateur section was also not easy to find and deserves its own main menu icon.

SPECIAL FEATURES

News contains more feature articles than breaking stories and has a weekly round up of the week's action titled Golf Notes.

Tours contains all the Rankings, Money Lists, Statistics and Schedules for the professional game. This section also contains Profiles of the top players on both sides of the Atlantic, although they don't appear to be updated regularly.

The Online Shop has News about the latest golf equipment and a strong Tuition section, which features two entire Tuition Series

overall rating:	★ ★ ★
classification:	news, info, tuition
updated:	regularly
navigation:	★ ★ ★
contents:	★ ★ ★
readability:	★ ★ ★
speed:	★ ★ ★ ★
UK	

as well as the usual Hints & Tips. The Shop section was more disappointing at the time of writing. Some of the sub-sections were still under construction and others just provided links to other online retailers of clothing, books, videos and equipment such as www.easygolf.co.uk or www.amazon.com.

The Clubhouse is open to both Visitors and Members. Membership costs £25 per annum and confers discounts on selected merchandise, as well as discounted green fees and specialised golf tuition. Visitors can browse through a Library of reference material, check out the rules of golf, or find details of a golf course in Course Directory. The Amateur golf section can also be found in Clubhouse. This contains news and calendars for events on the UK amateur scene, as well as details of Unions, Links, would be Playing Partners, and an invitation to become a virtual Roving Reporter for your club or area.

OTHER FEATURES

Travel contains more News articles, a limited number of golf course reviews, and links to providers of golfing holidays. The Notice Board has a message forum in Talk Back and an opportunity to have questions answered in Your E-mails, as well as Competitions and Links to other golf sites. Golf Radio is in the sub-menu on the left of the screen and provides a link to listen to The Golf Guys, an American radio show. Industry contains News and a Directory of companies involved in the golf industry.

A general golf site with an impressive scope but, as yet, a lack of depth to its content.

miscellaneous

www.golfcourses.org
Golf UK Ltd and Shared Knowledge Systems Limited

This is a useful resource for any travelling golfer looking for a course in the area he or she is visiting. The number of courses listed is impressive but the site would rate higher if more of them had been reviewed.

The design is smart and professional and navigation refreshingly simple. The main menu is uncluttered and runs down the left of the page. Clicking on the maps to find a course is well thought through.

SPECIAL FEATURES

Course Finder has three ways of finding course. You can either look at a Featured Site, or search for a Course/Club by typing its name, or click on a map of Britain for the Region of your choice. You can narrow your choice down first by county and then by town. In the entry for a particular club, you will find address Details, Course Details, Facilities offered, Membership Information and a Map. The Hotels section was still under construction at the time of writing.

overall rating: ★ ★ ★
classification: information, news
updated: regularly
navigation: ★ ★ ★ ★ ★
contents: ★ ★ ★
readability: ★ ★ ★
speed: ★ ★ ★ ★
UK

Course Reviews relies on readers to send in their thoughts on a course and, although the reviews listed are useful, there are not enough of them to make up a really meaningful resource.

OTHER FEATURES

Pro Shop was still under development at the time of writing, but does have some useful links to online retailers. You can get online quotes for your golf gear in Golf Insurance.

A useful resource for the golfer on the move.

www.mrgolf.com
Mr Golf Etiquette's website

This is a gloriously silly site and one of the funniest golf sites on the web. Mr Golf Etiquette (alias writer Jim Corbett) takes a wry look at not just the impossibly complicated rules of good manners on the course, but also the psychological trauma of being a bad golfer. You can't help but laugh out loud.

SPECIAL FEATURES

Enter The Prose Shop contains several literary sections about the vexed question of what constitutes good golf etiquette. You can have your questions answered in a humorous way in Ask Mr Golf Etiquette, or bone up on the basics in The Golf Etiquette Primer. There are more humorous articles by the resident expert in Mr Golf Etiquette Whacks Eloquently, and articles not by him in Articles by Other Authors. The Really Good Golf Jokes section is exactly what it says.

Enter the Pro's Shop A chance to buy some of Mr Golf Etiquette's print books or wacky merchandise such as tees and hats.

The Golf Etiquette Game is a suitably spurious way of whiling away an idle moment. Guess from the photo which rule of golf etiquette is being flouted and win a Mr Golf Etiquette hat. Wow.

Mr Golf Etiquette's Links are, naturally, well chosen.

Lively, silly, and the funniest golf site on the web.

overall rating:
★ ★ ★ ★

classification:
humour

updated:
monthly

navigation:
★ ★ ★ ★

contents:
★ ★ ★ ★

readability:
★ ★ ★ ★

speed:
★ ★

US

overall rating: ★ ★ ★
classification: Tiger Woods
updated: regularly
navigation: ★ ★ ★ ★
contents: ★ ★ ★
readability: ★ ★ ★
speed: ★ ★ ★
US

www.tigerwoods.com
Tiger Woods

If you are a fan of Tiger Woods or are simply curious about the phenomenal record of the greatest golfer ever known, then this is the site for you.

SPECIAL FEATURES

All About Tiger contains everything you could possibly want to know about Tiger Woods. There is a Biography, College History, Quotes and the Tiger Tracker, which will tell you every score from every round plus every dollar ever made by the great man. And if that isn't enough, you can see the Tiger Line, which details his progress year by year to the top of the sporting world.

Club Tiger is a free fan club, where you can post emails, read exclusive columns, take part in competitions, and read Tiger's Tips.

Tiger Watch has news stories and archived articles, photos, video footage and audio interviews, as well as Tiger's position in the Tour stats and money lists.

Off The Course has details of the Tiger Woods Foundation, a charity which encourages young people to achieve their potential.

A homage to a great sportsman, which manages to convey genius without being boastful.

motorsports

general

overall rating: ★ ★ ★ ★ ★
classification: news, results, comment
updated: frequently
navigation: ★ ★ ★ ★ ★
contents: ★ ★ ★ ★ ★
readability: ★ ★ ★ ★ ★
speed: ★ ★ ★ ★

www.autosportmag.com
Autosport

This is a very impressive, professional online motorsport resource, which scores both in its depth and breadth, as well as the sheer quality of its content. This really is a one-stop-shop for all of your motorsport needs. The site's red and black livery has a classic autosport feel, and it is a joy to navigate. There are two main menus. At the top of the screen there is a menu for the special areas of the site, while the main menu for different motorsports lies just below the title.

SPECIAL FEATURES

Database In the menu at the very top of the screen, this leads to a fantastic, searchable archive of the first six placed drivers in every Grand Prix ever held since 1950. You can also search for winners of the Drivers and Constructors Championships.

Radio is an online station, which broadcasts every Tuesday after a Grand Prix at 20:00 BST. If you miss the live show, you can catch up on race analysis plus interviews with big names from F1 in the audio archive. You will need a copy of RealPlayer to listen.

Email news is a daily news email service, delivered direct to your desktop, although you do have to hand over your address and car details to BMW.

F1 is by far the biggest section within Autosportmag, and can be found in the main menu just below the title masthead. Here there are Headlines and a neatly presented Standings and Results service. Profiles allows you to click on a driver or a team to find comprehensive biographies, race histories and a year-by-year story. Circuits contains both a map and historical detail.

Race Reports has a lap-by-lap account of every Grand Prix, as well as full results, race news and headlines. The Gallery contains a pictorial story of all the Grands Prix in the most recent season.

Features has several interesting sections. You can have your F1 questions answered in Ask Nigel (Autosport's Grand Prix editor), read Q&A interviews with F1's top stars, or read Adam Cooper's comprehensive race analysis.

Calendar allows you to click on a date to see what is happening in any motorsport, not just F1, on that given day.

OTHER FEATURES

You can read Headlines, Standings, Profiles and Race Results for CART, Rally, NASCAR, DTM, BTCC, F3000 and F3. The Cart section has the added bonus of a Features area, which includes a regular column from current driver Dario Franchitti. ALMS, Sportscars and IRL have a headlines-only service.

A superbly professional site, which holds the pole position for its breadth, depth and quality of content.

sport

overall rating: ★★★	
classification: news, comment, stats	
updated: frequently	
navigation: ★★★	
contents: ★★★★	
readability: ★★★★	
speed: ★★★	
US	

www.motorsport.com
Motorsport

This site is particularly strong in its coverage of North American motorsport, but not so extensive for Formula 1. Motorsport is an excellent resource for fans of the CART series in particular.

The design is modern and user friendly. Navigation can be a little fussy, as there are rather too many sub-menus on the left of the page. The main menu is easier to navigate, with clear section headings running across the page just below the title.

SPECIAL FEATURES

News has an understandable bias towards American motorsport, and is much better for CART, IRL and NASCAR than it is for F1. This section is searchable by motorsport category or by region, and is subdivided further into news and features sections. The latter contains a good range of interviews and comment.

Magazine contains more interviews and feature articles.

Photos has an extensive gallery of snaps from North American race meetings.

Compete boasts a fun prediction game called Pick 6, where you try to forecast the top 6 places in F1, CART, IRL and World Rally races. There is no prize money, 'just bragging rights', as Motorsport puts it.

OTHER FEATURES

The Statistics section has a good database of the results of CART races, although downloads of both RealPlayer and Acrobat Reader are required. The F1 stats section is a link to the redoubtable but frustrating Forix (see p.133).

A good resource for North American motorsport.

formula 1

overall rating: ★ ★ ★ ★ ★	
classification: analysis, comment, news	
updated: weekly on Wednesdays	
navigation: ★ ★ ★	
contents: ★ ★ ★ ★ ★	
readability: ★ ★ ★ ★ ★	
speed: ★ ★ ★ ★	
US	

www.atlasf1.com
ATLAS F1

This site is a fantastic source of thoughtful comment and analysis on Formula 1, and will appeal to any fan who has become jaded by a diet of pure news and results feeds. Formed in 1995, Atlas F1's writers are drawn from all over the world, which gives the site a global community feel. They are also all very readable. Atlas F1 welcomes contributions from readers, although the editor cannot guarantee that they will be published.

The style of the site might be weighty and sonorous, with its commanding double dragon masthead, but that does reflect the general seriousness of the content. Navigation takes a bit of working out as most of the content is on the homepage, which acts much like a newspaper front page. The main menu, just under the titles on the homepage, tends to lead to more minor sections.

SPECIAL FEATURES

Front Page contains a superb amount of thorough, well-informed comment on every aspect of Formula 1. Just click on the titles in bold and underlined in yellow to go to your section of choice. Review has authoritative analysis on recent races and events. Columns contains rumours, book reviews and quizzes.

You can read in-depth interviews and articles in Exclusive, or browse through cartoons and more analysis in Commentary.

2000 Season is where you can review WC standings, Driver Biographies and Teams Portfolios, which contains car specs, team history, and links to official sites.

Features is an excellent historical resource. There are pen portraits of the great and the good in F1 Hall of Fame, and a quick description of every year since Formula 1 began in 1950 in F1 Timeline. You can review accident stats and see how safety regulations have evolved in Safety in F1 or see the answers to The FIA 66 FAQ.

News Room is the place to go if you want more detail on the recent headlines. This section contains headline and archived news articles from Reuters, as well as selected audio recordings in The Sound of History. You will need a copy of RealPlayer for the latter. You can find more specific stories and results for all 17 races of the most recent season in The 2000 Season News Links. The news archive is fully searchable by keyword or month.

Bet Your Nuts is a free and addictive prediction game, in which you use your supply of cyber peanuts to bet on the outcomes of races. The first prize is a very worthwhile trip to one of next season's Grands Prix.

OTHER FEATURES

Bulletin Board has lots of active forums, but you will need to register for free before joining the members-only Paddock Club. Registration is also required for the Chat area.

Bookstore is run in association with www.Amazon.com, with editorial input from Atlas F1 in their recommendation section.

Search & Archive is an interactive search service providing access to every article, news report or feature ever published by Atlas F1.

Serious, analytical Formula 1 coverage with a global community feel to it.

www.planetf1.com
Planet F1 and the 365 Network

Planet F1 and the 365 Network conjure up their usual mix of news, comprehensive statistics and comment, producing a compelling resource for Formula 1 fans. Perhaps all this site really lacks is a top columnist from within the Formula 1 scene.

The site has a buzzing but clear design, and is a joy to navigate, with a well-organised menu down the left of the screen

SPECIAL FEATURES

2000 Results is an amazingly comprehensive database for every race of the season. For each Grand Prix, there is a Full Race Result, Race Report, Picture Gallery, Weather report, Previews, a Track Profile, Top historical Facts for the circuit, and a report on a Classic Race. You can also find out about Practice, Qualifying and Race Times, as well as reports from proceedings at the Daily Press Conferences, Drivers Quotes and Team Quotes.

Drivers 1950-2000 has an entry for every driver who has ever raced in a Grand Prix, with race statistics and biographies.

Head to Head is a facility for directly comparing two drivers' records against each other.

Teams 1950-2000 contains a history and car specification for all of the current teams, and an archive from Alfa Romeo to Zakspeed with everything in between.

overall rating:	★ ★ ★ ★
classification:	news, stats, comment
updated:	regularly
navigation:	★ ★ ★ ★ ★
contents:	★ ★ ★ ★
readability:	★ ★ ★ ★
speed:	★ ★ ★ ★
UK	

Circuits and 2000 Schedule give race tracks the once over. Every circuit has a map, a description of what it is like to drive the course, and results and records for every race held there.

Results Archive allows you to search the database by season or by individual Grand Prix, with a facility to see the year-by-year winners of the Drivers and Constructors Championships.

Breaking News contains all the latest headlines and an archive, searchable by keyword and date.

Picture Gallery has snaps from every recent Grand Prix.

Features has articles from a strong team of experienced writers, of whom the most readable is New Zealander Eoin Young.

Technical Focus covers all the latest gizmos.

F1 Newsletters delivers all the latest news direct to your desktop. This can be either in the form of Planet F1 Weekly or a Planet Race Update over the course of a Grand Prix weekend.

OTHER FEATURES

The F1 Online Shop has a mixture of official merchandise, limited edition prints and die cast models, but can be a bit pricey. You can also play an F1 Trivia Game or a Caption Competition for small prizes. Finally, you can try your hand at Fantasy Spread Betting, which promises all the fun of high rolling betting without the risk.

A compelling mix of facts, figures and comment.

www.forix.com
Joao Paulo Lopes da Cunha

Forix is the F1 fan's anorak dream. Every fact that has ever been logged or recorded about every Grand Prix since 1950 is available on this site, and is presented in a mind-boggling variety of ways.

Navigation is a nightmare, though, with a random selection of lists presented at the top of the homepage, and the more ordered sections tucked away at the bottom. It is worth persevering, though, either to search out that elusive fact or to marvel at the work that has gone into producing this site.

SPECIAL FEATURES

1950-2000 This is the most organised part of the database, and you can find it to the bottom right of the screen. Once inside, you can search all Grands Prix by country and by individual race. There are also details of every circuit that has been used for a Grand Prix. The Drivers section is particularly impressive. For every driver who has ever taken control of a Formula 1 car, you can find out how many GPs he started or won, how many Championships he won, and how many Pole Positions, Fastest Laps and Points he gained. Then you can do the same thing for Makes of car or Engines used. For drivers there are additional sections such as births and deaths, or Side by side comparison of the careers of up to four different drivers.

overall rating:	★ ★ ★ ★
classification:	facts and figures
updated:	regularly
navigation:	★
contents:	★ ★ ★ ★ ★
readability:	★ ★ ★ ★
speed:	★ ★ ★
BR	

Drivers Championship is on the middle left of the screen. This section contains all the ranking tables since 1950 and the result of every race, as well as its entry list, starting grid and details of fastest laps.

2000 contains all the stats for the most recent Championship.

OTHER FEATURES

Forix has a vast photo gallery, which can be accessed via Photo Gallery: New! or Show your work in Forix or See also. There appear to be very few races which do not have an image of some sort. The Driver's Words section homes in on a particular race from the past and has quotes from the leading players of the time, including their reactions after qualifying and after the race. Statistics delves further into increasingly bizarre manipulation of the facts and figures. Here, you can assess who is the greatest driver of all time by the Wildsoft F1 Ranking or the Drivers Super-championship methods. Alternatively, you can look at the longest Sequences of back-to-back Wins or Pole positions. Finally, there are (mercifully brief) details of the F.3000 Championship and the chance to wish Happy Birthday to the Grands Prix drivers of the day.

Absolutely every fact and figure about every Grand Prix.

www.formula-1.co.uk
Online magazine from World MotorSport Ltd

This is a useful resource for the Formula 1 fan who wants a quick news and results service, although some of the links to the archive material had fallen into disrepair when we looked at it. The editorial content is quite limited, but there is some worthwhile analysis in the Parc Ferme section.

The design is snappy and navigation simple, with a clear main menu down the left of the screen.

SPECIAL FEATURES

Parc Ferme is the most thoughtful and thought-provoking section of this site. It contains editorial items, race and driver analysis, and feature articles.

News has all the latest stories and an Archive section.

Results has a section for every race of the season. These contain track maps, race results, qualifying stats, and a list of winners going back as far as 1950.

Statistics contains a complete results Archive from 1994, along with standings, tables and details of fastest times recorded in Testing sessions.

Images has a well-stocked gallery for each race of the season.

overall rating:	★★★
classification:	news, results, analysis
updated:	frequently
navigation:	★★★★
contents:	★★
readability:	★★★
speed:	★★★★
UK	

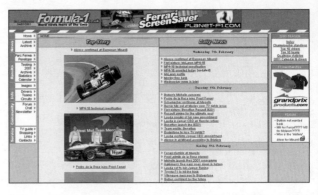

Info contains profiles of Drivers, histories of Teams, and descriptions of Circuits.

OTHER FEATURES

Community contains well-used Forum and Chat sections, courtesy of www.Delphi.com. Or you can choose to receive a weekly emailed Newsletter containing the latest news and results. Finally, Service contains UK TV motor sport listings, links to motor sport shopping sites, and a very large selection of motor sport Links.

Could do with more in it, but otherwise a snappy, simple-to-use news service.

www.itv-f1.com
ITV

This site has lots of strong points, in its well-written interviews and features, and its good library of photographs. But the site did not deliver on results, which were out of date, or on statistics, which were skimpy. The design has a clean, fresh feel, and the main menu on the left of the screen has a clear list of contents, Though half of this menu provides links to commercial partners.

SPECIAL FEATURES

Features contains a recap of the season so far, with some good action photographs. There are also interviews with drivers and team bosses, a column from Murray Walker, humour in Not the F1 News and dirt digging from an underground insider in Mole.

Results ITV-F1 claim to have up-to-date results, although at the time of writing all the results were from the 1999 season. However, this section does have some snazzy circuit maps.

News is sharply written, and there are in-depth reports throughout the season from the ITV Team.

OTHER FEATURES

There are pretty girls in Pit Babes, sharply written histories and car specs in Teams, and photos and biographies in Drivers.

Good for features and photos, not so good for results.

overall rating:
★ ★ ★

classification:
news, results, comment

updated:
regularly

navigation:
★ ★ ★ ★

contents:
★ ★

readability:
★ ★ ★ ★

speed:
★ ★ ★

UK

enthusiast

overall rating: ★ ★ ★	
classification: rumours	
updated: daily	
navigation: ★ ★	
contents: ★ ★ ★	
readability: ★ ★ ★	
speed: ★ ★ ★	
UK	

www.f1rumors.net
F1 Rumors online magazine

F1 Rumors is a fairly light-hearted site, devoted to peddling any story that leaks out of the Formula 1 garages. It is particularly useful for F1 addicts during the close season, when hard news tends to be thin on the ground.

The site is not very well laid out, with blocks of text appearing in awkward places and necessitating a lot of scrolling around. Navigation is simple if you stick to the main menu to the left of the screen. The smaller menu below the titles is less reliable.

SPECIAL FEATURES

F1 Rumors contains both team and technology speculation and is updated daily, or more frequently if the rumour mills are working at full stretch.

Rumors Archive has weekly batches of past mongering.

Silly Season This section comes into its own outside of the F1 racing season, when speculation on driver moves and technological advances is particularly rife.

F1 Articles has articles from non-professional writers looking at the sport from a fan's perspective. Some of the articles are beginning to look a bit dated, but the editors of F1 Rumors are keen for budding reporters to submit their own.

Mailing List is a free email service, which allows you to receive your rumours in a weekly or daily format.

OTHER FEATURES

F1 Live, F1 News, Betting, F1 Cartoons and Statistics are all links to sites with the relevant expertise in those areas.

A fun site for anyone who likes their news completely unsubstantiated.

motorcycling

overall rating: ★ ★ ★ ★	
classification: news, info, comment	
updated: regularly	
navigation: ★ ★ ★ ★	
contents: ★ ★ ★ ★	
readability: ★ ★ ★ ★	
speed: ★ ★ ★	
UK	

www.bikenet-racing.com
Bikenet Motorcycles Limited

This site contains a mixture of professional bike racing news and product information for the amateur rider. It will appeal to the armchair fan and enthusiastic participator alike.

The style is bold and readable, with a very clear main menu on the left of the screen. Bikenet's services for bike riders are in the menu at the top of the screen, just below the title masthead.

SPECIAL FEATURES

Racing is a link to Bikenet's sister site www.motorcycle-racer.com, which has all the latest news for World, British and AMA Superbikes, Road Racing, and Grand Prix Racing. Within the sections, you will find race reports and results, details of teams and riders, and in-depth news of the teams sponsored by Bikenet.

Road Tests and Product Tests Bikenet gives its verdict on the latest bikes and products here. The Features section has interviews with movers and shakers in the professional sport, as well as tips for better amateur riding.

OTHER FEATURES

In the main menu, you can join in Discussions or Chat with fellow enthusiasts, or bid for the bikes and accessories on offer in Auctions. In the services menu, you can buy a bike, consult a directory of suppliers, or get an insurance quote.

A valuable and readable resource for both bike riders and armchair fans.

sport

rallying

overall rating: ★ ★ ★	

overall rating:
★ ★ ★

classification:
reports and results

updated:
regularly

navigation:
★ ★ ★ ★

contents:
★ ★ ★

readability:
★ ★ ★

speed:
★ ★ ★

FIN

www.worldrally.net
World Rallying

This is a valuable specialist site, which will be of interest to any fan of the World Rally Championship. The stage reports are very comprehensive, and give a good insight into how each race progressed. The design is basic and navigation is simple in this relatively small site. Individual sections can be reached via the main menu on the left of the screen or through links within the homepage itself.

SPECIAL FEATURES

Reports contains accounts of all the World Rally Championship stages from the 1997 season to date. The reports tend to be factual rather than dramatic, but cannot be faulted for the amount of detail that they offer for each leg of each particular stage. In this section, you will also find results tables, current World Rally Championship Standings, and links to the official sites of the different WRC Events.

Profiles has a photo and brief career histories for all of the major Drivers in WRC, as well as information for the different Teams in the competition.

OTHER FEATURES

There are a selection of snaps from past rallies in Photos, a useful compilation of rally Links and a well-frequented Forum. News contains sporadic updates from the WRC.

A valuable, detailed archive of current and past stages in the World Rally Championships.

overall rating: ★ ★ ★
classification: news, results, statistics
updated: regularly
navigation: ★ ★ ★ ★
contents: ★ ★ ★
readability: ★ ★ ★
speed: ★ ★ ★
UK

touring cars

www.btcc.co.uk
British Touring Car Championship

This is a sound, if rather uninspiring site, which has plenty of detail and facts and figures for the Touring Car fan.

The design is in a garish purple, which does nothing for tired eyes, but navigation is well thought through. You will find a clear and direct main menu on the left-hand side of the screen.

SPECIAL FEATURES

Season contains detailed Preview, Qualifying and Race information for all 24 races in the 2000 Championship. It also promises a description of the various circuits, but the link was not working at the time of writing.

2000 Statistics has round-by-round analyses and point scoring for Drivers, Manufacturers and Teams, and details of the Michelin Cup for Independents and the Michelin Pit Stop Challenge.

Photo Library contains good photographic montages of the action from each venue.

Teams/Drivers has brief biographies plus links to the relevant official sites.

News Desk has some interesting stories from within and around the Touring Car scene.

Girl on Pole puts those glamorous grid girls in the glare of the media spotlight.

OTHER FEATURES

TV listings and a race calendar can be found in BTCC on TV, and Related Sites has links to other motorsport websites.

Masses of facts and figures for the Touring Car fan.

section 6
rugby

general

www.rugbee.com
Rugbee online magazine

This site was still very young when visited, but shows every sign of becoming a valuable addition to the world of online rugby news and comment. The editors of Rugbee have taken the unusual step of covering both rugby codes equally, although this does reflect how close rugby union and rugby league are becoming. The site's outstanding feature is the number of star players who have signed up to provide exclusive interviews, and pre- and post-match comment.

The site has a gold and black theme to reflect the 'bee' of the Rugbee title. Navigation is not as simple as it might be, mainly because the key areas of the main menu are placed towards the bottom left of the screen. Scroll down to get to them.

SPECIAL FEATURES

The homepage, or main page as it is known here, can be reached by clicking on the Rugbee logo in the top left of the screen. The striking line up of Rugbee players are each represented by a thumbnail photo. Clicking on any one of them will lead to the latest interview with that player. There are around 20 players, who include League stars Andy Farrell and Denis Betts and Union top performers Martin Johnson and

overall rating: ★ ★ ★
classification: interviews, news, comment
updated: regularly
navigation: ★ ★
content: ★ ★ ★
readability: ★ ★ ★ ★
speed: ★ ★ ★
UK   R

Austin Healey. Other, more occasional, interviews can be found by clicking on the box titled Look Who's Buzzing.

Chat requires free registration, but provides access to the players when they're online, for live interrogation.

Audio contains weekly, radio-style interviews with players. These were very few at the time of writing, although many more are promised. You will need a copy of Windows Media Player to listen.

Union News has all the latest match reports and comment from international matches and the Zurich Premiership.

League News provides the same service for Super League and the Rugby World Cup, with the added bonus of a column from the respected Dave Hadfield of the Independent.

Clubs enables you to search for news from the club of your choice.

Fitness Tips and comment on Strength, Speed, Endurance and Nutrition from fitness consultant and Rugbee founder Andrew Clarke. There are also animated Union Drills from Tacklesport.

OTHER FEATURES

Gallery has lots of action photos. Betting, Games and Merchandise are links to www.sportingodds.com, www.midassport.com and JJB Sports respectively.

A good site for getting an inside view from top players in both Union and League.

union

www.planet-rugby.com
Planet Rugby incorporating Rugby 365

The merger of the Planet Rugby and Rugby 365 websites has resulted in this comprehensive resource of news and statistics, which will appeal to all general rugby fans. Planet Rugby also has some very big-name columnists on its books, who provide interesting and hard-hitting comment on every aspect of the game. They are also way ahead of the field with their massive, interactive RU database, which leaves no blade of rugby grass uncovered. The site is home to the famous Planet Rugby World Rankings, and it is quick, slick and easy to navigate.

SPECIAL FEATURES

World Rankings are given pride of place in the top left of the screen, and a click reveals that the top three nations are all Southern Hemisphere teams. No surprises there, but England were ranked fourth at the time of writing.

Players/Records Located in the main menu, this section leads to an absolute feast of rugby trivia. The database contains records for over 10,000 international players and boasts entries 'for every recorded player who has ever played international rugby'. Just type a name into the relevant box and all the playing statistics come up. There is also an interactive search facility for

overall rating:	★ ★ ★ ★ ★
classification:	news, comment, archives
updated:	frequently
navigation:	★ ★ ★ ★ ★
content:	★ ★ ★ ★
readability:	★ ★ ★ ★ ★
speed:	★ ★ ★ ★
UK	

Rugby Milestones, and Records and Players by Scoring Averages. Archive 1871-2000 is a similarly formidable resource and contains an archive of results and reports on any international match played anywhere in the world since 1871.

Columnists Planet Rugby's writers are an extremely noteworthy bunch. Christian Cullen, David Herbert, Martin Johnson, Michael Lynagh and Stephen Jones of The Sunday Times all pen regular, readable articles for the website.

OTHER FEATURES

Latest News is bang up-to-date, and there is also an option to have daily or weekly news mailed to your desktop in Free E-mail News. Upcoming fixtures and an archive of results and match reports are available in International Fixtures and International Results. Photo Gallery has a great archive of action shots from recent internationals.

There is an opportunity to poke fun at figures in the contemporary game in Rugby Lookalikes as well as the chance to download rugby-themed Screensavers. The Rugby Shop has links to a selection of on-line retailers and the Rugby Search Engine provides links to other rugby websites. Finally, if you are still hungry for information, you can search for news archives by both Country or Tournament.

A bright, slick, comprehensive and very readable rugby resource.

www.gwladrugby.com
Gwlad Welsh Rugby Supporters

This site has masses to offer the Welsh rugby fan, and enough of a tongue in its cheek to make it entertaining for the English enemy too. The presentation is very slick and professional for an enthusiasts' site, and a lot of care has been taken to make navigation as easy as possible. It's great fun as well.

SPECIAL FEATURES

Homepage has a frequently updated digest of all the latest news relating to Welsh rugby. Contributors vary, but it is all freshly written from a fan's point of view, and pulls no punches in its criticism of players or administrators. There are also some useful links embedded in the text, which lead to the online sources of the news material if more detail is required.

Offside on the centre right of the screen, leads to some funny and inventive cartoons. Here's Jonny is an amusing spoof diary with 'exclusive reports from inside the England camp'. The Mark, found in the main menu on the left of the screen, leads to an online magazine, written by Welsh fans, packed with views and wry comment from the stands.

OTHER FEATURES

Latest Results from both the Welsh and English leagues are handily displayed on the homepage, with links to current league

overall rating:	★ ★ ★ ★
classification:	news, comment, humour
updated:	frequently
navigation:	★ ★ ★ ★
content:	★ ★ ★ ★
readability:	★ ★ ★ ★
speed:	★ ★ ★ ★
UK	

tables. Poll results are summarised in Gwlad Awards 2000, there is more humour in Big Dai, and Video Shop and Book Shop link direct to rugby related products at www.Amazon.com. A lively forum can be found in Chat.

Fixtures, results, match reports and league tables for all rugby involving Welsh international or club sides can be found in Wales, League, Cup and Europe respectively. Lions has tour and travel info for the 2001 British Lions tour of Australia.

Social has details of Gwlad's outings and events and Shop has a link to an online outlet for rugby shirts and other merchandise. TV Guide has listings for upcoming rugby programmes, Trivia is a quiz with prizes, and rugby books are given the once over in Review. Finally, if you have ever had the embarrassment of finding yourself humming along to those Welsh Rugby anthems, help is at hand in Songs, where all the lyrics can be found.

A fresh, funny and very slick look at the world of Welsh Rugby from a fan's point of view.

www.scrum.com
Scrum – part of the Sportal network

This website will appeal to any general rugby union fan, scoring well in the vast breadth of its coverage. Scrum seems to have a small army of journalists beavering away worldwide to bring you up-to-date news, scores and comment. It also packs in a heavyweight selection of star columnists, with regular articles from top current players and broadcasters.

SPECIAL FEATURES

Navigation by Country/Tournament leads to an impressive global resource for rugby union news, results, tables and fixtures. Scrum has contributors in all of the rugby playing countries of the world and the By Country section takes you globetrotting from Argentina to the USA via the big north and south hemisphere rugby nations. By Tournament is largely a different way of accessing the same information, but it is handy if you want to home in quickly on stats and comment for, say, South Africa's Currie Cup.

Columns Scrum's star columnists are an impressive bunch too. You can read articles and opinions from current players Lawrence Dallaglio, Andre Vos and David Wilson, as well as broadcasters John Taylor and John Inverdale.

Player Profiles has a useful picture and potted playing history for all of the world's current international players. Some of these have been interviewed in Star Q & A's.

overall rating:
★★★★

classification:
news, comment, live scores

updated:
frequently

navigation:
★★★★★

content:
★★★★

readability:
★★★★

speed:
★★★★

UK

Fitness has a complete training programme, which should be more than enough to satisfy every social player. If you're very creaky it's worth reading the warning though, before embarking on too demanding a routine.

OTHER FEATURES

Breaking news from around the world is dealt with in News Extra, with more depth and archive articles available in Scrum Features. A comprehensive, worldwide fixture list can be found in This Month's Fixtures and Test Fixtures, while Tours has the other upcoming international information. The women's and students' game is given a thorough work out in Women's Rugby and Student Rugby, and the Clubhouse is a great place to post your Social Calendar and Events Diary.

Posters offers you a chance to win recent posters from great rugby moments, and the Webcam gives a live opportunity to see what's going on in Murrayfield stadium. TV Guide has rugby-related listings for global TV, Rugby Primer is an idiot's guide to Rugby Union rules and Dictionary contains a glossary of all those confusing rugby terms. Finally, there is a comprehensive Links section, and a chance for you to air your own views in Bulletin Board and Reviews.

A magnificent breadth of worldwide coverage, if not quite with the depth of its rival Planet Rugby.

www.rugbyclub.co.uk
Zurich Premiership

Fans of any side in the Zurich Premiership will find a lot to enjoy in this site. There are sharp insights in the Preview and Features sections, as well as some comprehensive, up-to-date statistical Records. Navigation has not been very well considered, though; annoyingly, several different links lead to the same place. The better sections in Rugby Club are on the right-hand side of the screen with links highlighted in red.

SPECIAL FEATURES

Ref's Corner is an illuminating peek into the world of the referee in the high octane environment of the Zurich Premiership.

Preview takes a comprehensive look at next weekend's action under the authoritative gaze of the BBC's Alastair Hignell.

Features has topical articles from top journalists such as Brendan Gallagher of The Daily Telegraph.

Email News delivers your club's news and match previews regularly to your desktop.

Interviews is in the centre of the screen and offers in-depth reports of conversations with the players of the moment.

Select Team leads to the meat of the website. Here you can access squad details, fixtures, results, records and club information for the team of your choice.

overall rating:	★★★★
classification:	news, scores, comment
updated:	frequently
navigation:	★★★★
content:	★★★★
readability:	★★★★★
speed:	★★★★
UK	

Records has a particularly useful tool which lets you see how your club has performed Head to Head against any other club from 1987 to date.

Player Search Situated in the main menu on the left of the screen, this is the site's most fun section. Type in the name of any player who has appeared in the top flight since 1987 and all of his domestic and international records will come up.

OTHER FEATURES

On the right of the screen, Quick Links leads to potted fixtures, results and standings. Live Sky Matches has TV listings and Rugby Club Poll gives you a chance to vote on a topical issue.

In the main menu on the left there are other Fixtures & Results and Tables sections. Pocket Guide gives a round-up of Zurich Premiership rules and regulations, and Stats has the same information as can be found via Select Team above. Fun & Games links to Trivia365, an interactive quiz site. Chat Archive has details of old online question and answer sessions. To enter the Media Centre, you will need to register as a professional journalist.

A sharp site for the Zurich Premiership fan.

www.rfu.com
Rugby Football Union

This site will appeal to all followers of English rugby at every level. It has a particularly large and well-stocked online shop.

SPECIAL FEATURES

Rugby Store has a fantastic selection of rugby merchandise including books, clothing, souvenirs and equipment.

Elite Players can be found within the England section in the main menu and has informative pen pictures on top international players.

Clubs contains a massive, searchable database of fixtures and results for every professional and amateur league in England.

England Programmes Links to www.eventprogrammes.com, online retailers of new and back issue match day programmes.

OTHER FEATURES

The England section also has team news, fixtures and results, as well as a Discussion forum. Twickenham has details about the rugby museum and other facilities at the stadium. Finally, the Referees section enables the men in black to keep up to speed with latest law developments, via a discussion forum.

A valuable site for England fans and rugby shoppers.

overall rating:	★ ★ ★
classification:	news, results, info, shopping
updated:	regularly
navigation:	★ ★ ★ ★
content:	★ ★ ★
readability:	★ ★ ★
speed:	★ ★ ★
UK	

sport

overall rating: ★★★	

classification:
information, news

updated:
frequently

navigation:
★★★

content:
★★★

readability:
★★★

speed:
★★★

UK

www.sru.org.uk
Scottish Rugby Union

This is a useful site for the Scottish rugby fan and player, with some good information on both the international team and youth rugby. It is easy enough to navigate but the design is a little cluttered.

SPECIAL FEATURES

International is a good resource for making an online purchase of tickets for Scotland matches. Locations contains map directions to Murrayfield, while Squad has well-written pen pictures for all of the current Scotland international players.

Kids leads to Scruff, a great area for young Scottish rugby players and fans. There are lots of competitions with some good prizes, including a chance to become a Scotland mascot. What's On has a list of youth fixtures and social events and the DO's Pages has contact details for youth rugby Development Officers. There is also a regular Player Interview.

OTHER FEATURES

Pro Teams, Districts and Clubs has some limited fixtures and news information. You can learn more about the work of the Scottish Rugby Union in SRU.

A good first port of call for the Scottish rugby fan.

Rugby Union Clubs - Official Websites
2000/1 Season

Zurich Premiership

Bath www.bathrugby.com
Bristol www.bristolrugby.co.uk
Gloucester www.gloucesterrugbyclub.com
NEC Harlequins www.quins.co.uk
Leicester Tigers www.tigers.co.uk
London Irish www.london-irish-rugby.com
London Wasps www.wasps.co.uk
Newcastle Falcons www.newcastle-falcons.co.uk
Northampton Saints www.northampton
saints.co.uk
Rotherham www.rotherhamrufc.co.uk
Sale Sharks www.salesharks.com
Saracens www.saracens.com

Welsh-Scottish League

Bridgend www.bridgendrfc.com
Caerphilly www.caerphillyrfc.co.uk
Cardiff www.cardiffrfc.co.uk
Cross Keys none at present
Ebbw Vale ebbwvalerfc.co.uk
Edinburgh Reivers www.edinburghreivers.com
Glasgow Caledonians www.scottishrugby.com/
The Reds/Llanelli www.scarlets.co.uk
Neath www.neathrfc.co.uk
Newport www.newport-rfc.co.uk
Pontypridd www.pontypriddrfc.co.uk
Swansea www.swansearfc.co.uk

league

overall rating:	
classification: news, scores, comment	
updated: frequently	
navigation:	
content:	
readability:	
speed: ★ ★ ★ ★	
UK	

www.playtheball.com
Sportal – Rugby League

Sportal's playtheball.com is a good source of information and comment for every Rugby League fan, with a strong team of writers and refreshingly clear navigation and design.

SPECIAL FEATURES

Features is a good source of informed opinion about the latest issues surrounding Rugby League. Their star writer is the informed and always readable Andy Wilson of The Guardian. Ex-player Graeme Bradley has some outspoken views on the game, and the in-house writers also have their finger on the pulse.

SL Club Features is a good way of catching up on News, Squad members, Prospects and the History of the Super League clubs.

OTHER FEATURES

News Round-Up, Fixtures, Results & Reviews and Tables for the Super League, the Northern Ford Premiership and the amateur competitions. Challenge Cup covers the knockout competition. History describes the evolution of Rugby League .

Plenty of news and comment for the Super League fan.

www.rugbyleaguer.co.uk
Rugby Leaguer Magazine

There is a lot for every Rugby League fan to enjoy in this website. The reporting is full and the columnists crunch into the tackle with some straight-talking comment. The design is a little garish, but navigation is simple enough.

SPECIAL FEATURES

French on Friday and **Martin Richards Weekend Preview** can both be found below the News Update section, and offer some considered opinions and analysis on the week's RL happenings.

Columnists is where you can read transfer gossip from Dave 'Nosey' Parker, hard hitting comment from Maurice Bamford, and forceful opinions from Willie Boot.

Match Reports is a great place to catch up on all the weekend's action. There isn't much analysis but the reporting is full.

OTHER FEATURES

Up-to-date news and results in News Update, Aussie News, League Tables, and Results & Fixtures. There is a Message Board and Links to all of the Super League clubs' official websites. There are some fun tests for small prizes in competitions.

A professional, punchy resource for RL comment, reporting and news.

overall rating:	★ ★ ★ ★
classification:	news, scores, comment
updated:	frequently
navigation:	★ ★ ★
content:	★ ★ ★
readability:	★ ★ ★ ★ ★
speed:	★ ★ ★ ★
UK	

sport

overall rating:	★ ★ ★
classification:	information, humour
updated:	regularly
navigation:	★ ★ ★
content:	★ ★ ★
readability:	★ ★ ★
speed:	★ ★ ★
UK	

www.rlsa.org.uk
Rugby League Supporters Association

This is a simple, fun site, and it will appeal to all general Rugby League fans. Its key features are a well-maintained link section and an amusing online magazine. The design is rather uninspiring and it is sometimes difficult to get back to the homepage, but otherwise navigation is simple enough.

SPECIAL FEATURES

The Greatest Game! or TGG! is a lively, online magazine with some fun features. Early Bath has humorous comment on all aspects of Rugby League, while TGG! Classics has a round up of the more contentious issues covered by the magazine. Pot Pourri has miscellaneous articles and the Aled Hardby column offers the spoof ramblings of a Rugby League fanatic.

League Link Central contains a comprehensive, well-organised, up-to-date list of worldwide Rugby League links.

OTHER FEATURES

Virtual Terrace is a lively chat forum, and RLSA sets out the aims of the Rugby League Supporters Association. There are also links to ticket outlets for major Rugby League tournaments.

A fun and useful site run by Rugby League fans for Rugby League fans.

Rugby League Official Club Sites

Super League 2000
Bradford Bulls www.bradfordbulls.co.uk
Castleford Tigers www.castigers.com
Halifax Blue Sox www.bluesox.co.uk
Huddersfield Sheffield Giants www.giants
online.co.uk
Hull www.hullfc.com
Leeds Rhinos www.leedsrugby.co.uk
London Broncos www.londonbroncos.co.uk
Salford Reds www.reds.co.uk
St Helens www.saints.uk.com
Wakefield Trinity Wildcats www.trinitywild
cats.co.uk
Warrington Wolves www.wwrlfc.co.uk
Wigan Warriors www.wiganrl.com

section 8
tennis

official sites

www.rolandgarros.org, www.usopen.org & www.ausopen.org
French, US & Australian Open Tennis Championships

These three sites, like Wimbledon, are best viewed when the respective tournaments are in progress. The design for each site is modern and stylish, and though similar, each captures national identity well. They also all have clear and well-defined main menus, which makes for painless navigation.

SPECIAL FEATURES

Scoreboard contains details of completed matches by event, as well as match stats and a real-time scoreboard for following matches live. There is also a schedule of play and event stats, such as the number of aces. Draws has all the draws broken down into easily viewed sections.

News & Photos has all the latest reports plus interviews with players. These can be viewed in text or video, although you will need to download a copy of RealPlayer for the latter.

All the Players in a tournament are listed alphabetically. Clicking on a name reveals a photo, plus full biography, as well as links to related articles.

overall rating:	★★★★★
classification:	news, stats, interviews, info
updated:	frequently during tournaments
navigation:	★★★★★
content:	★★★★★
readability:	★★★★★
speed:	★★★★★
UK	

The **Live** and **Interactive** sections provide views of the courts and grounds via netcam, a fixed webcam, or slam cam, a robotic webcam which can be panned and zoomed at your leisure. These services are available only when a tournament is in progress. You can take a virtual tour of the various venues with the help of the above cameras or through photographic images. The Live and Interactive sections also have various fan polls, cyber postcards and downloadable wallpaper.

The **Roland Garros Live & Interactive** section has an area called ipix, which allows you to manipulate a panoramic view of Court Suzanne Lenglen with your mouse.

Live @ the Open is the US site section, and also contains a live audio broadcast service when the tournament is in progress, although you will again need a copy of RealPlayer to listen.

The history of the tournaments can be found in Roland Garros World, New @ the Open (US) and About the Open (AUS) respectively. The French site uniquely provides an opportunity to view video highlights of singles finals between 1990 and 1997. RealPlayer is again required.

OTHER FEATURES

Each site has a Shop section containing branded and other tennis merchandise. Costs of shipping will be prohibitive for UK purchasers from all but the Roland Garros site.

Slick, modern and very professional sites from IBM, which are a must when the respective tournaments are in progress.

www.wimbledon.org
All England Lawn Tennis and Croquet Club

A fantastic resource for any tennis fan, which really comes into its own when the Championships are taking place. Highlights include live score tickers, live video interviews, and webcams.

There are really two very distinct sites in one here, and the style of site varies between rather traditional and staid in the All England Tennis Club section, to bang up to date in the 2000 Championships site. Navigation is relatively simple in both sites with main menus at the top of the screen.

SPECIAL FEATURES

Championship Web Sites in the main menu provides a link to Launch the 2000 Championship Site. This is the heart of the web site and is at its best when the Wimbledon Championships are in progress. During the 2000 Championships, the site recorded 2.3 billion hits. On the homepage, during the tournament, you can find scores, results, draws, the day's schedule, weather forecasts and match reports. There is also an opportunity to listen to player interviews, athough you will need to download a free copy of RealPlayer before you can do this.

Info has details of how to obtain tickets, how to get to Wimbledon, the history of the Championships and the Museum.

News has more match reports, feature articles and interviews, as well as a photo gallery of the top tennis personalities.

---

overall rating:
★★★★★

classification:
live action, info, stats

updated:
during tournament

navigation:
★★★★

content:
★★★★★

readability:
★★★★★

speed:
★★★★★

UK

Scores allows you to search a database of completed matches by event, and view match statistics. During the tournament, you can also download a Live Scoreboard. Competitor List contains all of the players' names and clicking on any one of them leads to a more detailed Player Profile. Event Stats has details of the best servers and worst double faulters, as well as more general tournament stats.

Wimbledon Live is a great interactive service, but you will need a copy of RealPlayer to use most of it. You can watch live player interviews, listen to match commentary, view images from live webcams dotted around the grounds, go on a virtual tour, watch archived video footage of classic matches, get scores on your mobile phone, or play a daily trivia quiz.

OTHER FEATURES

Back on the Wimbledon site, you can buy clothes, bags, books, videos, gifts and towels in the Online Shop, or find out about ticket prices and how to enter the ticket ballot in Tickets.

There are details of the Championship's history and organisation in Wimbledon Info, and a glimpse into the archives in Museum. The Video Vault again requires a copy of RealPlayer to view clips of great matches, interviews, and a musical slide show in 2000 Montage.

A busy site that's absolutely at the heart of the action while the Championships are taking place.

www.atptennis.com
ATP tennis tour

This is an efficient, well thought-out site, which has a good mix of statistics, personal information and fun activities. It will appeal to any fan of men's tennis.

Navigation is very simple with a main menu on the left-hand side of the page. The design of the site is fresh feeling with different colour coding for each section. There is a good selection of action photos on most pages and the speed of downloading is quick despite the high graphic content.

SPECIAL FEATURES

News & Scores has up-to-date coverage of every event on the tour. All the latest match news can be found in Scores and Draws. Or, if you prefer, you can receive updates direct to your desktop in Newsletter, which also has an interactive menu so that you can customise what you receive.

Players is the superbly comprehensive statistical section of the website. Player Profiles takes you straight to the page of the player most in the news at the moment. Here, and for every other player on the tour, you can find personal details, where he stands in the Champions Race (the ATP annual rankings), and career performance information.

His Activity goes into an even greater level of detail. For every player for every year since 1990 you can find out how much prize

overall rating:	★ ★ ★ ★
classification:	news, statistics, fun
updated:	frequently
navigation:	★ ★ ★ ★ ★
content:	★ ★ ★ ★
readability:	★ ★ ★ ★
speed:	★ ★ ★ ★
US	

money he has won, who he has beaten and to whom he has lost. Players also has a section for Head-to-Head career stats. For an overall look at who is up and who is down, you can click on Race Leader Board, ATP Doubles Race or the inelegantly named Sortable Race.

Tournaments contains current and historical information for every event on the tour. Clicking on Tournaments itself brings up pages for the current and next events or you can plan out the whole year in Full Calendar. Event History is an interactive database for every ATP tournament since 1990, while the junior tour is covered in Challengers.

OTHER FEATURES

Fanzone has a lively chat room and a Your Letters page. You can also send a message to your favourite player on Fan Board or access more fan sites in Fan Links.

Inside The ATP is a mainly administrative section but it is worth checking out for competitions with prizes in Promotions.

ATP Tour Shop is a link to www.tenniswarehouse.com, a California based tennis e-tailer. They will mail purchases anywhere in the world but beware high transport costs.

A brisk, fresh feeling site with lots of useful information.

www.wtatour.com
Women's Tennis Association

This site is a very useful resource for any fan of women's tennis. It is not quite as full and comprehensive as the men's ATP Tour site but there is still a lot of news, stats and biographical detail on over 1000 current players.

The site is modern in design with tennis ball icons to click on in the main menu. Overall navigation is quite simple, although the splitting of the main menus between the top and bottom of the screen can be a bit confusing at first.

SPECIAL FEATURES

Tournaments contains a list of all the tournaments on the year's WTA tour, with details of individual events. This section also has worldwide TV listings in tour TV guide, and a weekly newsletter rounding up the action in notes and netcords.

News & Scores has the latest news by headline with a link to the whole article if required.

Players has a list of all the competitors on the LTA tour which are searchable alphabetically. Clicking on a name leads to a good amount of additional information, including rankings, career highlights, potted biography and personal details. The player profiles section in Players has a photo and more biographical information on one of the hot players of the moment. One to Watch performs a similar service to young players working their

overall rating:	★ ★ ★ ★
classification:	news, stats, information
updated:	regularly
navigation:	★ ★ ★
content:	★ ★ ★ ★
readability:	★ ★ ★ ★
speed:	★ ★ ★ ★
US R	

way up the rankings, and player guide is an online opportunity to buy the WTA's print brochure of the same name.

Rankings All the current stats with a singles and doubles standings database, searchable alphabetically or by nationality.

Get To The Point can be found on the homepage and enables you to receive an email update of news from the WTA Tour. You need to complete a free registration form first.

History is in the menu at the bottom of the screen and contains details of past rankings leaders, top money earners, and Grand Slam Tournament winners going back to 1975.

OTHER FEATURES

The Pro shop has a limited number of items for sale including calendars, T-shirts and hats. Links has click-throughs for other official tennis websites.

In Tennis Talk in the menu at the bottom of the screen, you can post your views on Message Board or talk to other tennis fans in Chat, although you will need to register first. Off the Court contains information about the WTA's Player Development Program, which is designed to introduce tennis to a new generation of players. Multimedia has a WTA promotional video but it proved very slow to download.

An up-to-date and very useful resource for any fan of women's tennis.

www.daviscup.org
Davis Cup

This is a brief and to the point site, which provides an excellent point of quick reference for anything and everything to do with the Davis Cup.

The design is direct and functional with an easy-to-navigate main menu, which includes drop-down sub-menus all contained down the left of the page.

SPECIAL FEATURES

Results contains details of the current tournament and draws for the next tournament, as well as results for each year going back to 1995.

Teams has biographies and career information for the players involved in the big matches. There is also an interactive archive where you can search the database to see how countries and players have fared against each other.

Interactive has some good competitions in Gamezone, where prizes include tickets and trips to top Davis Cup matches. You can listen to play in progress on Live Radio, although you will need to download RealPlayer first. Finally, you can see a fan's eye view of a match on the 360 degree camera, which pans around a venue.

overall rating:	★ ★ ★
classification:	news, results, stats
updated:	regularly
navigation:	★ ★ ★ ★
content:	★ ★ ★ ★
readability:	★ ★
speed:	★ ★ ★ ★

sport

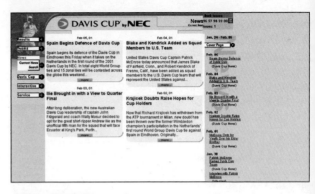

OTHER FEATURES

Davis Cup contains a history of the tournament and its Rules &
Regulations. Services has information about the Location of
matches as well as ticketing advice and TV schedules. The latest
headlines can be found in Current News, which also contains an
archive searchable by keyword.

A neat quick reference site for Davis Cup news, results and stats.

www.lta.org.uk
Lawn Tennis Association

This site has a very broad range of content and has something to interest both the tennis player and the tennis fan. The design is upbeat but often tries to cram too much information onto a page, which leads to a lack of direction, an accusation that some might level against the LTA in general.

The main menu is clear and lies down the left of the screen. Navigation gets more difficult once you are in a particular section, with some very long, cluttered pages, which are hard to negotiate. Some of the sections would definitely benefit from a clear sub-menu.

SPECIAL FEATURES

LTA Online Shop leads to a special section of sports e-tailer www.sweatband.com. Here you can buy rackets, shoes, balls, clothing and accessories with substantial discounts for LTA members and County Club Card holders.

News has the latest on how British players are faring in ATP Tour events, as well as Davis Cup and LTA Tournament news. You can also cast your vote for the LTA annual awards, and catch up on the various LTA tennis initiatives going on around the country.

Fans Zone contains a page for each of the top male and female British players. On these, you will find a photo, biographies and detailed career records for every year they have been on the circuit.

overall rating:
★ ★ ★

classification:
news, information

updated:
regularly

navigation:
★ ★ ★

content:
★ ★ ★ ★

readability:
★ ★

speed:
★ ★ ★ ★

UK

Fans Zone also has a weekly update of major events, world rankings, British Player Rankings and British Player Whereabouts on the tennis circuit.

Players Zone has loads of information for people wanting to take up tennis, emphasising the junior game. Here you can find out about such tournaments as Girobank Tour for budding pros, and the LTA Junior Championships. There are also details about Play Tennis, an LTA initiative to get youngsters onto the courts.

Coaching Zone has information about the LTA Coaching Scheme for aspiring coaches. There is lots of detail on how to get on courses, how to become a coach and how to work your way up the LTA coaching ladder of qualifications.

Clubs Zone will help you find which one of the 2,300 tennis clubs affiliated to the LTA is closest to you, as well as giving tips on how to run a tournament or build a tennis court.

Schools Zone has plenty of information on how to get kids started playing tennis, how to keep them playing, and how they can make it all the way up to being a pro.

OTHER FEATURES

Ace Magazine has details of how to subscribe to this print publication. Web Links has some useful pointers to other tennis sites, and About LTA describes the organisation's work.

A lot of useful information for fan and player alike but it is not an easy site to find your way around.

news

www.tennis.com
Tennis Magazine

This site is an online offshoot of the US-published Tennis magazine. It has some useful news, tips, and fitness sections but the very American bias may not be to all tastes. The main content from the last month's print Tennis magazine can be found by clicking on the magazine cover on the homepage. The main menu runs down the left of the page and is easy to navigate.

SPECIAL FEATURES

News has the latest from the professional circuit in Hot Headlines as well as a Results and Scores section.

Equipment is a reference and review facility for all the latest fads and technological advances, with dispassionate reviews of kit and equipment in Search Racquets and Search Shoes.

Fitness contains all the latest tips for outwitting your opponent through training and nutrition. You can also learn about the top players' punishing routines in Workouts of the Pros.

Instruction More ideas and tips for improving your game.

A brash, very American view of the tennis world with some good tennis tips and equipment reviews.

overall rating:	★ ★ ★
classification:	news, information, tips
updated:	regularly
navigation:	★ ★ ★ ★
content:	★ ★ ★
readability:	★ ★
speed:	★ ★ ★ ★
US	

miscellaneous

overall rating:	★ ★ ★ ★
classification:	news, info, results
updated:	monthly
navigation:	★ ★ ★ ★ ★
content:	★ ★ ★ ★
readability:	★ ★ ★ ★
speed:	★ ★ ★

www.gbtennisgirls.com
British Women's Player Committee

British women's tennis might not be the most successful area of UK sport at the moment but it has certainly made an impact with this website, compiled by the Women's Players Committee. There is plenty of player information here, as well as reports of how the girls are getting on (often very well) in the smaller tournaments, which are not always covered in the mainstream media. It also offers a fascinating insight and advice into what it is really like to be a professional tennis player.

The site has an appealing design and lots of content. It is very easy to navigate with a straightforward main menu down the left-hand side of the screen. It can, however, be a little slow to download pages containing lots of graphics.

SPECIAL FEATURES

Player Profiles has biographies and career details of the 30 British players represented by the Women's Players Committee. These include such items as a photo, rankings information and interviews. You can also email a player from here.

Resource Centre is a fantastic source of information for both budding pros and their parents. Here you can find out everything from good schools for tennis, to LTA player schemes, to what hoops need to be gone through before you can enter your first professional tournament.

News/Results gives all the latest tournament draws and results plus a round-up of how the girls did in the big WTA tournaments.

Chat posts up dates and times when players will be available for live question and answer sessions, although they were rather out of date at the time of writing. You will need to register first.

Message Board contains more thoughtful questions, comments and replies than is common on the message boards of most other websites.

Events Calendar lists the events in the British tennis season from the lowliest Challenger tournament right up to Wimbledon. It also indicates the ticket price.

Player Gallery has a smattering of photos of our girls in action.

OTHER FEATURES

Sponsors contains information on how to sponsor a player. This can be done for a little as £12 in the 100 Club, which also offers the opportunity to win your money back plus a little more via a sweepstake. On the homepage, there is a Player of the Month section and a link to the hottest news article.

A mine of information for both fans and budding players of women's tennis.

overall rating: ★ ★ ★
classification: fan site
updated: regularly
navigation: ★ ★ ★ ★
content: ★ ★ ★
readability: ★ ★ ★
speed: ★ ★
UK

www.henmagic.freeserve.co.uk
Sarah Vickery's Tim Henman fan site

This homage site to Tim Henman cannot help but win you over with its sheer enthusiasm. The style is a rather crazy mix of competing typefaces but navigation is straightforward. There is a main menu on the left of the page and links to Sarah Vickery's other tennis sites at the bottom. Joining the fan club costs £15 for a year's membership and entitles you to a free magazine five times a year, as well as photos and posters.

SPECIAL FEATURES

Photos 1999 and **Photos 2000** contains thousands of images of Tim Henman in action around the world. Copies can be ordered online with payment accepted in sterling, $US or $Aus.

News has a day-by-day account of Tim's activities and Results 2000 has details of every set Tim has played this year.

OTHER FEATURES

Sarah Vickery also runs websites for Jan Michael Gambill, Mariano Zabaleta, Nicholas Lapentii, Greg Rusedski and Andre Agassi. Messages can be sent to any of the players on the Message Board. Chat Room is open at 9pm BST every Wednesday for Tim fans.

A spectacularly enthusiastic homage to Tim Henman and other tennis players.

other sports

american football

overall rating: ★ ★ ★ ★
classification: news, stats, comment
updated: frequently
navigation: ★ ★ ★ ★ ★
content: ★ ★ ★ ★
readability: ★ ★ ★ ★
speed: ★ ★ ★ ★ ★
US

www.nfl.com
Official Site of the National Football League

Sports which generate a lot of statistics often make for great websites and NFL is no exception. Here you can search through a mind-boggling number of stats, and compare teams and players in thousands of different ways. There are great audio and video sections too.

The site is bold and bright with two main menus. News and stats for the NFL as a whole can be found across the top of the screen, while more specific items are in the menu which runs down the left.

SPECIAL FEATURES

NFL Films is a great way of catching up on gridiron action. Here you can watch reviews and previews, listen to trainers screaming from the sidelines in Sound Trax, or simply re-live the latest Superbowl. The Team Theater section on the right of the screen tailors recent action for your favourite team.

NFL Insider is where you'll find in-depth news and comment in text format.

Stats can be found in the menu at the top of the screen. It includes 2000 interactive databases, Rosters, Depth Charts,

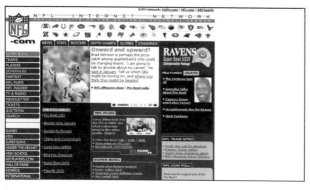

Scores and Standings. The menu on the left allows you to narrow this information down for Teams, or you can search through an alphabetical list of Players for season stats and biographies.

OTHER FEATURES

There are three free games to play in Fantasy (registration required) and a free email Newsletter service, which you can tailor to your favourite team.

A very professional, news, stats, audio and video service.

archery

overall rating: ★ ★ ★
classification: news, results, info
updated: regularly
navigation: ★ ★ ★ ★
content: ★ ★ ★ ★
readability: ★ ★ ★
speed: ★ ★ ★
UK

www.gnas.org
Grand National Archery Society

This is a compact site, which packs in a lot of information behind a simple homepage and is a great resource for both current and prospective archers. The design is a little homespun but the main menu on the left of the screen is clear and easy to navigate. There is a smaller menu at the top right of the screen.

SPECIAL FEATURES

How To... is a useful section for anyone interested in taking up archery. Here you can find information on how to locate your Local Club, Archery Society and Coaching Organiser, as well as how to join GNAS.

News has reports on how UK archers have been faring in competitions. Events contains an interactive Online Tournament Diary, which is searchable by month and has the option to Add your own Event to the list. If you want more information about an Event then click on its Title.

The Shop contains badges, ties, coaching aids, the GNAS magazine and archery accessories, all purchasable online.

There is a very comprehensive Links section, containing over 1100 Clubs and Associations.

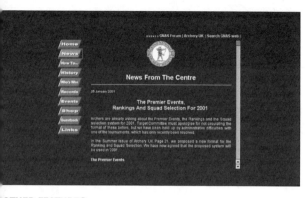

OTHER FEATURES

You can discuss the archery issues of the day in GNAS Forum,
subscribe to the GNAS quarterly magazine in Archery UK, review
UK National Records and Rounds in Records, and find out who
are GNAS's great and good in Who's Who.

A useful resource for current or prospective archers.

athletics

overall rating: ★ ★ ★ ★	
classification: tips, information	
updated: weekly	
navigation: ★ ★ ★ ★ ★	
content: ★ ★ ★ ★	
readability: ★ ★ ★ ★ ★	
speed: ★ ★ ★ ★	

www.kicksports.com
Kick!

Kicksports is a great self-help resource for the amateur runner, packed with information from how to choose the best shoes to preparing yourself for the big race, and is written in an engaging style. Navigation is simple, with the menu at the left of the screen.

SPECIAL FEATURES

New Runner contains everything you need to know to get started. Good Running has lots of great tips on how to improve , and you can work up to peak performance in The Big Race.

Gear has guides to getting yourself equipped. Aches & Pains contains pointers for self-diagnosis of those troublesome injuries. A runner's diet is covered in The Kitchen. Finally, you can use the Running Log to help you track your progress.

OTHER FEATURES

There are forums in Running Club, US race listings in Calendar, and readers' accounts in Virtual Races.

Everything an enthusiast could want to know about starting and improving their running.

www.onrunning.com
Onrunning online magazine

This site has a good mix of running news, comment and tips, which will appeal to both armchair fans and active participants. The homepage contains Commonwealth Gold Medal winner Peter Elliott's Training Camp section of the website. You can have your email questions answered in Ask Peter, get a Tip of the Week, learn how to Pace Your Race, or gain information on conditioning, health and nutrition. The link to www.myhealthscore.co.uk just below the titles leads to an interactive questionnaire to assess your levels of health.

The style is bright and breezy and navigation is well thought-out. The Site Map is in dark blue on the left of the screen, while special sections can be found in the pink area on the right of the homepage.

SPECIAL FEATURES

Special Features has an intriguing area called Future Stars, which has a weekly focus on an outstanding junior athlete, although frustratingly there was no archive facility.

Online Shopping offers clothes and accessories, and 20 per cent off selected branded sportswear.

overall rating:	★ ★ ★ ★
classification:	news, info, comment, tips
updated:	regularly
navigation:	★ ★ ★ ★
content:	★ ★ ★ ★
readability:	★ ★ ★ ★
speed:	★ ★ ★
UK	

OTHER FEATURES

The Bupa Events and General Events sections contain reports from major meetings such as the Olympics and the Great North Run. Running Fitness contains articles from the print magazine of the same name. There are comprehensive News, Fixtures and Results sections.

A useful resource for both armchair fans and active runners.

www.iaaf.org
International Amateur Athletics Federation

overall rating:	★ ★ ★
classification:	news, results, info
updated:	regularly
navigation:	★ ★ ★
content:	★ ★ ★ ★
readability:	★ ★ ★
speed:	★ ★ ★
MO	

Sites from sports administration bodies can be a little stuffy, so it is a pleasant surprise to find that the IAAF have found a good balance here between news stories, results and interviews, and the usual 'Speeches from the President'. There is a clear menu on the left of the screen, though some of the terminology is unusual, such as Exchange Zone instead of 'Links'.

SPECIAL FEATURES

Live Now links to the most recent events.

Results contains details and standings from the Grand Prixs and Golden League, as well as an Archive of World Championship results. There are also comprehensive Records and details of best performances of the year for each event in Top Lists.

Multimedia Interviews with athletes after major events in both video and audio (you will need RealPlayer), and a Photo Gallery.

OTHER FEATURES

News has a good range of stories from around the world. The Sport contains an introduction to athletics and its events plus some serious, in-depth Special Features articles. Inside the IAAF outlines the history and aims of the organisation.

A good source of athletics news, results and comment.

badminton

overall rating: ★ ★ ★	
classification: news, results, comment	
updated: regularly	
navigation: ★ ★ ★	
content: ★ ★ ★ ★	
readability: ★ ★ ★	
speed: ★ ★	
UK	

www.worldbadminton.net
World Badminton online magazine

This site has semi-official status, as it has close links to the International Badminton Federation. It is a very useful resource for any fan of top flight badminton.

The site has a simple, unassuming design with some dramatic photographic images on the homepage. Navigation is via a main menu running across the top of the screen. Run your mouse pointer over the main menu to open a drop-down sub-menu within each section.

SPECIAL FEATURES

News is searchable for the last week, fortnight or month. There is also an interactive facility for searching the International Badminton Federation (IBF) Archive. On the homepage, you can click on Join List to sign up to receive free email news updates.

Results has scores, draws and full reports from the major international tournaments.

Rankings contains all the current standings plus an explanation of how they are compiled.

Features offers interviews with top players, coaching tips and a special section for Sydney 2000.

Player Profiles is another interactive search facility. Type in the name of a player to find a photo and a playing record.

OTHER FEATURES

Competitions provided an opportunity to win Sydney 2000 memorabilia at the time of writing, while Events contains a calendar of upcoming tournaments.

A solid news and information service for fans of international badminton.

baseball

overall rating: ★ ★ ★ ★ ★	
classification: news, stats, live action	
updated: frequently	
navigation: ★ ★ ★ ★	
content: ★ ★ ★ ★ ★	
readability: ★ ★ ★ ★ ★	
speed: ★ ★ ★ ★ ★	
US	

www.majorleaguebaseball.com
The Official Site of Major League Baseball

This is another all singing, all dancing American sports site, which is absolutely packed with information. It also has some exciting innovations, particularly in its Baseball Live section.

The site has a bright design and is quite easy to navigate, despite the main menu on the left of the screen being very long and detailed. The menu across the top of the screen, just below the titles contains statistics and information for the whole of Major League Baseball, while individual team stats can be accessed via Clubs on the left.

SPECIAL FEATURES

Baseball Live (Shockwave Player required) is in the Live Coverage section and is an impressive multimedia experience for watching the sport. Here you can watch a game unfold complete with animations of the action, live scores, live text commentary, and live statistical analysis. There is also an opportunity to chat to fellow online audience members. The rest of Live Coverage has Daily Video highlights, Live Game Audio (either RealPlayer or Windows MediaPlayer required) and Wire Photos direct from the stadiums.

In the menu at the top of the screen Stats leads to a mass of information for every player in the League, including how they compare for Hitting, Pitching and Fielding. However, if that proves too insubstantial, you can also use something called the Baseball Stats Explorer, an interactive tool to break down those vital figures still further.

Clubs is in the menu on the left of the screen and allows you to home in on your favourite Major League team. Here you will find information on Schedules, Results and Injuries, as well as News, Stats and Video Highlights of the most recent action.

Store contains a massive amount of merchandise for every team, including clothes, books, collectibles and accessories. However, there was no international shipping at the time of writing so you will need a pal in the USA to take delivery for you.

Fantasy is also accessible via a link above the titles. It is the official Fantasy Baseball Game and is free to enter.

OTHER FEATURES

MLB Info (left menu) has lots of background detail for Major League Baseball, including Official Rules, History/Records, and Archives. Events contains all of the important baseball diary dates, and Community has a Fan Poll, Fun & Games and a Kids section.

A complete online resource for everything to do with top pro baseball.

basketball

overall rating: ★ ★ ★ ★	
classification: news, stats, comment, live action	
updated: frequently	
navigation: ★ ★ ★ ★ ★	
content: ★ ★ ★ ★	
readability: ★ ★ ★ ★	
speed: ★ ★ ★ ★ ★	
US	

www.nba.com/uk/
National Basketball Association

This is a slick, professional, multimedia machine from the NBA, which is stacked full of facts, figures and video/audio highlights. It is worth using the UK suffixed URL to tailor news for the UK, although all other content is common to NBA.com. The UK homepage is part of the NBA.com Global Basketball section and brings you NBA news from a UK perspective, including the latest from the British-born players, Steve Nash, John Amaechi and Michael Olowokandi.

The site's style is bright and breezy with lots of photos. Navigation is via a straightforward main menu at the top of the screen, just below the titles.

SPECIAL FEATURES

Sight & Sounds has video and audio highlights (RealPlayer or Windows Media Player required). You can also sign up for an Audio League Pass, it costs $29.95 for a season and allows you to listen to all of the NBA games live, though some games are free.

Features contains player interviews while all the NBA facts and figures can be found in Stats & Schedules. You can also search for information on your favourite Teams or Players.

OTHER FEATURES

Chats & Mailboxes has details of when your favourite players will be online to answer your questions. The NBA store is packed full of goodies ranging from personalised jerseys to collectibles, but international shipping rates start at a substantial $20.

Slickly presented basketball news, features and live audio.

sport

overall rating: ★ ★ ★	
classification: news, results, comment	
updated: regularly	
navigation: ★ ★ ★	
content: ★ ★ ★ ★	
readability: ★ ★ ★	
speed: ★ ★	
UK	

www.britball.com
Britball

Britball is a worthy, reliable site for the British basketball scene. The main menu has sections for the BBL, NBL Men and Women, Ireland and Scotland. There are also sections for the rival ULEB and FIBA European leagues, as well as the Saporta Cup, NEBL and England Men's national team. In each of these you will find results, standings and schedules, plus brief match reports. The style is a tad bland, and there are no graphics, but this can be forgiven since the site collects a lot of information about British (and European) basketball, which is simply not available anywhere else.

SPECIAL FEATURES

Profiles Team information for the BBL Conferences, and the bigger clubs in the NBL and Irish League. There are also very brief playing histories of top players and coaches.

Features contains in-depth articles and interviews. You can receive email news by signing up for free to News by Email.

OTHER FEATURES

There are basketball forums for you to air your views in The News Wire and in Hoopchat.

A reliable if uninspiring information source for British basketball.

boxing

www.boxingtimes.com
The Boxing Times

This is a small site which punches well above its weight for the sheer pizzazz of its writing and downright enthusiasm for its subject. It's hard to imagine taking boxing reports from any other source again.

The design is understated compared with the content. Navigation is via the dozen or so links on the homepage.

SPECIAL FEATURES

Fight Analysis Boxing Times writers' verdicts on all of the big fights. This can be a riot of colourful prose, packed with hyperbole. But who cares when you can read lines like this: '...it was the theme song of the one-sided contest, and the puzzled Ruiz could never name that tune. Instead, he ate leather and got busted up.'

Columns If anything the action gets even more bizarre here. Only in America could you find a boxing columnist who also doubles up as a Catholic priest. But the Texan Father Steve Sellers has an equally thrilling writing style. It's very funny too.

Fight Breakdown contains some very in-depth, round-by-round analysis of recent fights.

overall rating:	★★★★
classification:	boxing news & comment
updated:	monthly
navigation:	★★★★
content:	★★★★
readability:	★★★★
speed:	★★★
US	

OTHER FEATURES

Monthly Contest is a monthly prize draw for boxing memorabilia prizes. World Rankings has all the ups and downs for the IBF, WBC and WBA. Boxing Gallery has limited edition boxing prints for sale.

Hilariously over-the-top fight reports and comment.

www.world-boxing.com
World-boxing

There is a lot of useful information and informed comment on this
site, which will make it attractive to any fan of British boxing, with
columnists including Barry McGuigan. However, being essentially
a Frank Warren magazine there is a disproportionate amount of
puff and hype devoted to his stable.

SPECIAL FEATURES

Audio & Video allows you to view interviews, workouts, and
weigh-ins. Quick Time 4 is required.

Features contains some well-written build-ups to big fights. Fight
Facts has boxing records, and Weight Classes allows you to view
the historic greats in each division. Champions lists the current
champs for the WBC, WBA, IBF and WBO at every weight.

Fight Specials gives an in-depth treatment to a handful of the
most recent big heavyweight contests.

OTHER FEATURES

Press Releases and Stable of Fighters allow you to catch up on
who's hot in the Frank Warren empire. Latest News has a great
selection of daily news stories.

*A good multimedia news and comment service for British boxing
fans.*

overall rating:	★ ★ ★ ★
classification:	magazine
updated:	regularly
navigation:	★ ★ ★ ★ ★
content:	★ ★ ★ ★
readability:	★ ★ ★ ★
speed:	★ ★ ★
UK	

cycling

overall rating: ★ ★ ★ ★	
classification: news, live action, archive	
updated: frequently during race	
navigation: ★ ★ ★	
content: ★ ★ ★ ★	
readability: ★ ★ ★ ★	
speed: ★ ★ ★ ★	

www.letour.fr
Tour de France

This is an invaluable resource for any fan of the Tour de France, which is at its best when the race is in progress. It is, however, worth checking back at other times to see the route of next year's Tour, or to relive the detail of previous races.

The design is bright and colourful and makes good use of photographic images. There are no main menus, as such, on any of the pages – the links appear within the pages themselves. Navigation is relatively easy, although it is difficult to return to the Letour homepage without using the Back button.

SPECIAL FEATURES

The 20 stages of the 2001 Route of the Tour from Dunkirk to Paris can be viewed either in Flash or a conventional version. You can click on a stage for a description of the start and end towns. The leader's jerseys and the breakdown of prize money are explained in The Stakes, and you can see the full enormity of the obstacles in Mountain Stages.

You can relive all the stages of Lance Armstrong's triumph in Tour de France 2000. For every stage, there are minute-by-minute race developments in News Flashes, a race report, a

Route Profile and Standings. This is the Live part of the website, which you will be able to use when the 2001 Tour is in progress.

When a rider's name is underlined, you can click on it to find his full Tour history and a rather bald collection of career details. There is also an opportunity to Meet the Winner of a stage via the post race press conference. You will need a 56k connection to see a video or a 28k connection to listen only. RealPlayer (and usually some European language skills) are required for both options.

Finally, you can see a full 3D, panoramic representation of the course using Terra Explorer. Clicking on GO 3D enables you to go on an Interactive Flythrough of a stage's major landmarks. You will need at least a 56k connection and to download Terra Explorer before you can do this.

There is a similar amount of detail in English for the 1996-99 events in All the Tours on the homepage. Or you can search the historical database, an interactive archive containing all the race stories and riders' histories since 1903.

OTHER FEATURES

The Boutique is accessible via the Tour de France 2000 section though none of the replica jerseys were available when we visited. However there were stocks of accessories and a selection of books and videos.

A huge information resource, which really comes its own when the race is in progress.

darts

overall rating: ★ ★ ★ ★	
classification: news, results, info	
updated: regularly	
navigation: ★ ★ ★ ★	
content: ★ ★ ★ ★	
readability: ★ ★ ★	
speed: ★ ★ ★ ★	
UK	

www.planetdarts.co.uk
The Professional Darts Corporation

This is a neat, compact website from The Professional Darts Corporation. It will have a broad appeal for any fan of the pro darts scene. The site has a bold 'red top' design, which gives it the feel of a tabloid newspaper. Navigation is simple: click on the main menu just below the masthead, choose from the Quick Links just below, or click on any of the links within the homepage.

SPECIAL FEATURES

News contains match reports, full draws from tournaments and interviews with star players.

Players has profiles of the top eighty or so men and women (but predominantly men) players. You will find a playing history and a brief biography for each.

Statistics has Rankings details for the top fifty male players in the world, plus an explanation of how the Rankings are compiled. You can see the Women's World Ranking Top ten, as well as the Men's, as a permanent fixture on the homepage.

Diary has listings information for the major upcoming tournaments.

OTHER FEATURES

A link to Planetdarts' online darts game can be found on the homepage. Use your mouse to aim and throw the virtual arrows.

Online Shopping is also on the homepage. Shirts, caps, limited edition signed dartboards, flights, pins and souvenir programmes and videos are available.

A compact, reliable source of information for the pro darts scene.

equestrianism

overall rating: ★ ★ ★	
classification: news, results, features, info	
updated: regularly	
navigation: ★ ★ ★	
content: ★ ★ ★ ★	
readability: ★ ★ ★	
speed: ★ ★ ★	
UK	

www.equestrian.co.uk
eQUESTRIAN online monthly magazine

This is a great site for catching up on a wide range of equestrian sports activities. It will appeal to both the armchair fan and the active participant.

The design is a little cluttered and some of the type is very small but the content more than makes up for these failings. The main menu is on the left of the screen, but it is worth searching around on the homepage for special features and links.

There are sections for Showjumping, Endurance, Dressage, Driving Trials, Riding Clubs and Pony Clubs. Within each of these, there are News articles, What's On, Results, and Ranking Tables. By scrolling down and looking on the right of the homepage, you will find more special sections. Features has in-depth articles on topical items, and Vicky's Verdict is opportunity to have your email questions answered by top eventer Vicky Collins.

SPECIAL FEATURES

News is in the main menu and is indexed by the FEI, BHS, and BEF. You will also find sections on Point to Point, Horse Shows and Hunter Trials.

Resources has a Bookstore in association with www.amazon.com. The Press Releases section brings you the best of current special offers on equipment and consumables.

OTHER FEATURES

Good links to other equestrian sites around the world, on the right of the homepage.

A super resource for equestrian sports fans and participants.

fencing

overall rating: ★ ★ ★	
classification: news, results, info	
updated: regularly	
navigation: ★ ★ ★	
content: ★ ★ ★ ★	
readability: ★ ★ ★	
speed: ★ ★ ★	
UK	

www.britishfencing.com
British Fencing Association

This is a great source of information for anyone interested in taking up fencing, and a good way of catching up on news and events for the active fencer.

The design has a rather unstructured feel and it is a shame that there are not more reports and photos to accompany the results. The main menu runs down the right of the screen, while links to individual international competition sites can be found on the left.

SPECIAL FEATURES

Start Fencing contains a history of the sport, a description of The Weapons (the foil, epee and sabre) and a Glossary. There is a quick history for kids in Junior Fencing. You can learn how to become a member and discover what benefits that brings in Membership. Clubs has a region-by-region guide to BFA affiliated clubs.

Results contains the standings from British tournaments and you can find out who is up and who is down in Rankings Lists. Competition has details of upcoming events.

Welcome to British Fencing

The OFFICIAL page of the British Fencing Association

There is an opportunity to subscribe to The Sword, the BFA's quarterly magazine. It costs £15 for four issues.

OTHER FEATURES

Information on how to join coaching courses in Coaching Programmes and safety advice in Technical Information.

Lots of info for the would-be fencer, plus results and rankings for the current fencer.

greyhound racing

overall rating: ★ ★ ★ ★	
classification: results, information	
updated: regularly	
navigation: ★ ★ ★	
content: ★ ★ ★ ★	
readability: ★ ★ ★ ★ ★	
speed: ★ ★ ★ ★	
UK	

www.thedogs.co.uk
British Greyhound Racing Board

This is a great site for anyone new to greyhound racing, or for those who are thinking of branching out into ownership for the first time. There is a timely results service and an excellent betting guide too.

The design is extremely classy with a luxurious green background and some great still photographs of dogs in action. Navigation is via a main menu, cleverly done out in the six colours worn by greyhounds in a race. Our only complaint is that it is impossible to return to the homepage without frantic use of the Back button.

SPECIAL FEATURES

Results & Betting has an invaluable guide to making informed wagers on greyhound racing, as well as results from around the country as they happen. Before you make your first visit, or perhaps every time you make a visit to a greyhound track, you should take time out to read the Guide to Betting. Here you can find out how to find a winner, how to read class and form, how to make your money work, and how to read racecards.

Track us Down has a map of all the greyhound tracks in the UK, plus directions, ticket information and details of big races.

Adoption & The Superstars has details of retired greyhounds who are looking for a family home to see out their retirement. The Superstars are the greyhounds in the Hall of Fame and other Big Race Winners.

Ownership is an invaluable guide to the whys, wherefores, do's and don'ts of being a greyhound owner.

OTHER FEATURES

It is worth clicking on the Six Pack promotion if you are planning a night out at the dogs. There are some great discounts for groups, including drinks and dinner offers.

A stylish site with some extremely useful content.

gymnastics

overall rating: ★ ★ ★ ★
classification: news, results, info
updated: regularly
navigation: ★ ★ ★ ★
content: ★ ★ ★ ★
readability: ★ ★ ★ ★
speed: ★ ★ ★
UK

www.baga.co.uk
British Gymnastics

This is a very well thought out site, which delivers an excellent blend of gymnastics news, results and information.

The site design is clear, bright and bold and has some good photographic images. The main menu or index runs down the right of the homepage.

SPECIAL FEATURES

All the details from recent big competitions, such as the Women's and Men's British Championships and Sydney Olympics 2000, can be found in the green panel on the left of the homepage. They contain results and well-written reports.

News is divided into two areas. Recent Press Releases can be accessed by pressing the flashing link just below the titles. More general news can be found in BAGA News in the main menu – this is an interactive section which can be searched by gymnastic discipline.

BAGA – Introduction and **BAGA Disciplines** contain a history of gymnastics and a description of the different disciplines.

Photo Gallery has images of Britain's (and the world's) finest

gymnasts in action. Past Champions has the complete role of honour for British Champions – from 1896 for Men and from 1924 for Women

OTHER FEATURES

Regional Organisations has contact details. The Community Network and Junior Gymnasts Area were both under construction at the time of writing but promise a better online service for the gymnastic community.

Lots of useful information presented clearly and concisely.

horse racing

overall rating:	★ ★ ★ ★ ★
classification:	news, results, tips, stats
updated:	frequently
navigation:	★ ★ ★ ★ ★
content:	★ ★ ★ ★ ★
readability:	★ ★ ★ ★ ★
speed:	★ ★ ★ ★
UK	

www.racingpost.co.uk
Racing Post

Racing Post is about as close as you can get to an online racing bible. The site is an absolute mine of racing facts, figures, analysis and tips, and effectively acts as several print newspapers rolled into one. The design is fresh and clear and makes good use of colour to get across lots of complex and detailed information. Navigation is also easy with a clear main menu running down the left of the screen.

SPECIAL FEATURES

Today's Racing has full cards, betting verdicts and a map of the course for all of the day's meetings. You can also click on a horse within an individual race card to see its full racing record. In addition, there is race-by-race Analysis, Meeting Information, Course Details, and a round-up of how all the Tipsters view the various races.

Yesterday's Racing has all the results and a commentary on how every horse performed. It all seems so obvious when you have the marvellous advantage of hindsight. Future Racing looks forward to meetings, again with the same remarkable level of detail. Past Results has full analysis of earlier racing.

Stats has yearly racing records broken down by Jockeys,

Trainers and Owners, and then by British Jump, British Flat, All Weather, Turf Flat, Irish Jumps and Irish Flat. These records go back in some cases as far as 1996.

Tipsters & Reports contains racing news articles, and tables which reveal the records of the various press racing tipsters. These can be viewed as the NAPS Competition, the National Press Challenge or as Racing Post's own Tipster Analysis.

Live Results has a pop-up window so that you can view all the results on your desktop as they happen.

OTHER FEATURES

Bloodstock gives loads of details about the various sales going on around the country. These include Features, Sales Catalogues and Sales Returns plus a statistical service in Progeny Results and Stallion Statistics.

Greyhounds contains News, Tips, Ratings information and a column from Michael Fortune.

Sports Betting has Tips and information for Football, Cricket, Rugby, American sports and special events.

Print Outs allows you to download race information. Cuttings Library allows you to search the Racing Post archive interactively.

Stable Tours Succinct, well-written biographies of trainers .

Statistics and tips heaven for racing fans.

sport

overall rating:	★ ★ ★ ★
classification:	fantasy game
updated:	daily
navigation:	★ ★ ★ ★
content:	★ ★ ★ ★
readability:	★ ★ ★ ★
speed:	★ ★ ★ ★

UK   R

www.fantasy-racing.co.uk
Fantasy Horse Racing

Here is a fun site for anyone who likes to test themselves against the bookies, but doesn't much fancy parting company with the folding stuff. It is all completely free and run by racing enthusiasts. You just need to register to obtain your £1000 of fantasy betting money (and password) and then enter the monthly competitions. The site has a neat design and navigation is via the main menu on the left of the screen.

SPECIAL FEATURES

The Rules of the Competition can be found in About Fantasy. There are three competitions, each with nominal prizes from sponsors. The first is a League with three divisions, Thoroughbreds, Handicappers and Platers. Everyone starts as a Plater and works their way up the Leagues through a monthly promotion and relegation system. If you find you are not doing so well in the League, you can try your hand at Daily Combo or at Daily Bismarck – in the latter you have to select losers. You can check your progress in Daily Report and make your selections in Play Today, or look in Hall of Fame for a list of monthly champs going back to 1995. Horses to Follow enables players to receive email notification of when a fancied horse is due to run. Bet Settler allows you to calculate those winning returns.

A very skilled and satisfying fantasy gambling game.

www.channel4.com/sport/racing_c4/
Channel 4

Channel 4 offer brief, very readable previews of the day's action plus some engagingly written feature articles, which will appeal to anyone new to the sport. The site has a clean, bright feel and is easy to navigate via the main menu at the top of the screen.

SPECIAL FEATURES

Morning Line is a companion section to Channel 4's TV show of the same name, and has a round-up of the day's action, plus tips, and an overview of the top stories in the daily press.

Info has dispassionate guides to betting, and getting the most out of watching racing, and profiles of top jockeys and trainers.

Update contains previews of big races, interviews with big names from the sport, a list of horses to follow, and guides to some of the more confusing aspects of the racing world.

Q-files is a history of racing and its more colourful characters.

OTHER FEATURES

Win has information on the competitions Channel 4 Racing runs. There are also biographies of the Presenters, brief descriptions of top Courses, and a Calendar of Channel 4 Racing's TV coverage.

A great introduction to racing.

overall rating:	★★★★
classification:	comment
updated:	daily
navigation:	★★★★
content:	★★★★
readability:	★★★★
speed:	★★★★
UK	

overall rating: ★★★★
classification: news, comment
updated: frequently
navigation: ★★★★★
content: ★★★★
readability: ★★★★
speed: ★★★★
UK   R

www.racetips365.com
The 365 Network

There are in fact very few tips on Racetips365. Instead, you will find racing information and some thoughtful articles and interviews. The style is crisp and clear, and navigation, as with all of 365's sites, is very simple. The main menu runs down the left-hand side of the screen. The tip of the day can be found in Today's Best Bet in the top right-hand corner of the homepage.

SPECIAL FEATURES

Features Here you can find in-depth jockey interviews by Peter Naughton, articles on assessing form by Mark Newman, informed betting market comment from Bruno Casciato, and an American Eye view from John P Grier. There are also links to Site of the Week, Races to Remember, and Horse of the Week.

News has all of the breaking stories plus Audio Features from www.sportonair.com. The Trainers and Jockeys sections contain photos and succinct pen pictures of the major players.

OTHER FEATURES

There is a full Results and Fixtures service plus Racecards. There are also Going Reports, a good selection of Racing Links and a powerful Racing Search Engine.

Informed racing comment.

www.thehorsesmouth.co.uk
Glance plc

Information not quite from the horse's mouth, but the next best thing, with frank assessments of horses' chances from around 50 trainers. The site has a bold, blokey style and is simple to navigate. The main menu is on the left, but the info from the trainers can be found in the box at the top right.

SPECIAL FEATURES

Today's Trainer Information Trainers with a horse running that day are highlighted in red. In most cases the information will be in the form of an audio interview plus text version.

Thehorsesmouth Daily column from in-house tipster Colin Brown, which includes a preview of the upcoming action, as well as an archive of recent interviews with trainers.

OTHER FEATURES

Trainers contains interviews and biographies of most of the country's top trainers. The News section also has some Features, which include betting plans and suggestions for horses to follow. The Racecards section requires free registration, which enables you to download daily cards.

Horse racing information direct from trainers.

overall rating:
★ ★ ★

classification:
tips, information

updated:
daily

navigation:
★ ★ ★ ★

content:
★ ★ ★

readability:
★ ★ ★

speed:
★ ★ ★

UK

sport

ice hockey

overall rating: ★★★★★	
classification: news, results, stats, info	
updated: frequently	
navigation: ★★★★★	
content: ★★★★★	
readability: ★★★★★	
speed: ★★★★★	
us	

www.nhl.com
Official site of the National Hockey League

This is a slick, multimedia site, which is packed with audio, video, charts, news and stats.

The design is clear and bright and the site is easy to navigate. There are two main menus, one on the left of the screen and the other across the top just below the titles.

SPECIAL FEATURES

Every NHL match is broadcast in Live Game Radio (in the menu on the left of the screen), for which RealPlayer is required. Or you can catch up on Video highlights of the most recent action – QuickTime required.

The left menu also has scores and match reports in Schedules, live scoring, stats and charts in Scoreboard, the latest Standings, and Team and Player info in Stats.

In the menu at the top of the screen, Lineups contains team sections, team news, stats and schedules, as well as biographies and playing histories for Players and Coaches.

World Game has reports on the European players in the NHL. Fan Central has a selection of Games and a Chat zone. Kids has

more Fun & Games for the Under 12's, and Lace 'Em Up has coaching hints and tips. The History, Rules and Hall of Fame for ice hockey can be found in Hockey U.

OTHER FEATURES

The Shop has lots of clothes, hats and collectibles and will deliver to the UK.

Slick, informative, responsive. Everything you could want from a sports news site.

olympics

overall rating:	★ ★ ★ ★
classification:	news, results, photos
updated:	now archive only
navigation:	★ ★ ★ ★
content:	★ ★ ★ ★
readability:	★ ★ ★ ★
speed:	★ ★ ★ ★
AUS	

www.olympics.com
International Olympic Committee

This is the official site of the international Olympic Committee, so if you're suffering withdrawal symptoms from Sydney 2000, you can check out Athens 2004, and the Winter Olympics planned for 2002 and 2006.

The site has a bright, engaging style. Navigation is straightforward with a clear main menu running across the screen just below the titles.

SPECIAL FEATURES
Salt Lake 2002 holds an enormous amount of information divided between committee-style updates, Olympic news, and information for the complete winter sports novice. If you're a winter sports fanatic, there's even an opportunity to become part of history in Get Involved, by either applying for a job or helping as a volunteer. Each winter sport has its own sub-section (found in the menu on the left) with comprehensive news, features, athlete biographies and interviews, and features on the history and rules of the sport. An impressive collection.

Athens 2004 The homepage appears in its native Greek, but clicking on the Union Jack in the bottom left-hand corner brings up the English version. This part concentrates more on the

Olympics as an institution than the Salt Lake 2002 section, although you can view a copy of the timetable and training schedules in the Sports section.

Torino 2006 There's obviously a limit to the amout of previewing that you can give to an event that is still almost six years away, but this section does a good job of presenting the background information. There's news on the ongoing organisation of the event and features on the Turin area.

Olympic Museum gives a unique insight into the history behind the modern Olympics. In Gallery you can take a virtual tour through the museum exhibits and learn the stories behind the objects on display. You can also view video clips of opening and closing ceremonies in Virtual Gallery, and read a potted history of each of the Games since 1896, in The Games.

OTHER FEATURES

Olympic Collectors reveals the art of collecting Olympic memorabilia. International Olympic Committee gives news on the organisation and aims of the games, and International Sports Federations gives the contact details for sports organisations from Bridge to Taekwondo.

A well-rounded site, which achieves the unenviable task of providing a comprehensive body of information for both sports bureaucrats and enthusiasts alike.

rowing

overall rating: ★ ★ ★
classification: news, links
updated: daily
navigation: ★ ★ ★
content: ★ ★
readability: ★ ★ ★
speed: ★ ★ ★
UK

http://users.ox.ac.uk/~quarrell/
The Rowing Service by Rachel Quarrell

This is an excellent starting point for anybody looking for online rowing information. Rachel Quarrell has scoured the web to bring you all the latest world-wide rowing news, results and press cuttings. The site is not especially pretty and some of the links are no longer working. However, for a free and non-profit making service, this is an impressively comprehensive site. The homepage has two menu links at the top, while the main menu resides in multi-coloured boxes below.

SPECIAL FEATURES

New Rowing Information Latest news, fixtures, results and information from around the world, updated daily.

Press Scrapbook has a collection of both in-house reports and the best rowing journalism from the major regattas.

OTHER FEATURES

Masses of links, ranging from Results and Events to Picture Links, a Juniors section, and the Cox Box.

Dip your oar here first to discover the world of online rowing.

sailing

www.quokkasailing.com
The Quokka Sports Network

Quokka cover several sports but their ocean sailing output is
worth a special mention. The site looks absolutely fantastic with
lots of action images on a cool, ocean blue background. The
content does not quite live up to first appearances with the
same items re-hashed in different sections – but the site is
worth a visit for the visuals and multi-media elements.

Navigation is straightforward with a clear main menu running
across the top of the screen. However, the menu titles are not
always very descriptive of content, and it is worth looking out for
the Events panel on the homepage, which has up-to-date, race
specific information.

SPECIAL FEATURES

At the time of writing the BT Global Challenge and The Vendee
Globe were being given in-depth coverage, with a 2D global map
Race Viewer available for the former.

Expert Eye contains race analysis and comment, while Athlete's
Voice has text and photograph reports from sailors at sea.

Chronicles has feature reports and photo montage stories from
major regattas, while Gallery (confusingly) contains video and

overall rating:	★ ★ ★ ★
classification:	news, reports, comment, images
updated:	regularly
navigation:	★ ★ ★
content:	★ ★ ★ ★
readability:	★ ★ ★ ★
speed:	★ ★ ★ ★ ★
US	

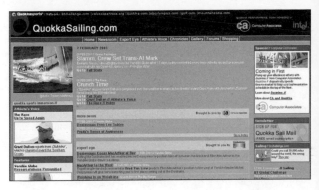

audio reports. You will need QuickTime or RealPlayer and preferably a broadband connection to watch the films.

OTHER FEATURES

Newsroom has updates from the major ocean racing. The shop has branded merchandise from the America's Cup, the BT Global Challenge, and the Volvo Ocean Race.

A great-looking site that is worth a visit for the visuals alone.

www.vendeeglobe.com
Vendee Globe

overall rating:	★ ★ ★ ★
classification:	news, multimedia, archives
updated:	regularly during race
navigation:	★ ★ ★ ★ ★
content:	★ ★ ★ ★
readability:	★ ★ ★
speed:	★ ★ ★
FR	

This is another of those sites that is clearly at its best when competition is in progress, but it also has some excellent archives of previous races. During the Vendee Globe 2000, the site was a multimedia heaven of video and audio reports, virtual boat tours, and online global boat positioning.

To get to the homepage click on the small Union Jack to the right of the title. This leads you to the main site, which has a funky design with lots of graphics, and is simple enough to navigate. There is a very clear main menu on the left of the page.

SPECIAL FEATURES

Radio/Film has on-board radio and video reports, while the Video of the Day can be accessed from the homepage. You will need RealPlayer and at the very least a 56kbps connection to watch the films.

News has up-to-date analysis of the state of the race plus a searchable archive of previous reports.

Positions gives the current rankings with the option of following the boats' progress in either a 2D or 3D map format. You will need to download software from Virtual Observer before viewing the 3D version.

Videos has interviews with the skippers and virtual tours of their boats, while Skippers has biographies of the competitors.

OTHER FEATURES

Weather Map contains forecasts for the whole of the Vendee Globe route and History contains some great video archive footage of previous races.

A superb online resource for following the race live, plus some good archive material.

snooker

www.snookernet.com
Snookernet

This is a well-designed, well thought-out, complete resource for any snooker fan or player. There are lots of scores and reports from the professional game plus a well-stocked shop, and a interactive tool for finding a snooker club in your area.

The site has a neat design and is easy to navigate. The main menu has clear titles and is conveniently situated just below the title masthead.

SPECIAL FEATURES

News & Results contains all the latest from the major tournaments. Diary & Rankings has very comprehensive tournament listings in Tournament Diaries, which include Pro-Am, Junior, Ladies and Billiards events as well as the Professional ones. Rankings has all the official Embassy Rankings plus a list of Modern 147 Breaks and Ladies and Billiards Rankings.

Interactive contains a Trivia Quiz and a Prize Contest, as well as a chance to have your email questions answered in Ask Snooki.

The Shop is well stocked with all sorts of snooker paraphernalia, from tables to balls and gifts. The Club Finder allows you to enter

overall rating:	★ ★ ★ ★
classification:	news, scores, shopping, club finder
updated:	regularly
navigation:	★ ★ ★ ★ ★
content:	★ ★ ★ ★
readability:	★ ★ ★ ★
speed:	★ ★ ★
UK	

a postcode to find a snooker club in your area.

Reference & History section includes an online Snooker Master Class from Terry Griffiths, brief Player Profiles, Snooker History and Rules.

OTHER FEATURES

Multimedia has a small photo gallery of snooker players and there is a well-maintained selection of links.

A neat site covering snooker from all the angles.

squash

www.squashplayer.co.uk
Squash Player

This is a superb resource for any squash player or armchair fan of the game. The site is absolutely packed with news, player details, results, rankings and photos, and also contains some high calibre reporting.

The design feels a little cramped and old-fashioned in places but navigation is simple. Just follow the main menu navigation bar at the very top of the screen.

SPECIAL FEATURES

Magazine contains Features from the print version, including player interviews and profiles. The Video and Book Shop are well stocked but there is no online ordering as yet. Squash Update is a free email newsletter.

Workshop has Clinics for Rules, Coaching and Fitness, and you can have your email questions answered by The Internet Squash Doctor.

News contains frequent tournament updates, illustrated with some very good photo galleries. Results has all the facts and figures from every major tournament. Events has calendars for international and domestic competition. Rankings has details

overall rating:	★★★★
classification:	news, results, comment
updated:	regularly
navigation:	★★★★
content:	★★★★
readability:	★★★
speed:	★★★
UK	

for the Top 20 men and women, as well as a Hall of Fame, Player Profiles and links to Players' own Sites.

OTHER FEATURES

Offers has prize competitions, Services has links to squash equipment suppliers, and there is a well maintained selection of Links. The Clubs section is an interactive database to help you find domestic and international squash clubs.

A complete online squash resource.

OTHER SITES OF INTEREST

Athletics

www.triathlete.com

This US site for the toughest of all athletic disciplines has feature articles on training and nutrition, as well as breaking news and an international triathlon calendar. There is also a well-used Chat and Message area, as well as a link to www.triathlonlive.com, another US site with more news, results and rankings.

Bowls

www.worldbowlstour.com

This is a useful, if not completely reliable, resource for any fan of professional bowls. The homepage takes an age to load because of an unwieldy Flash-based design, but once you are there you can find some timely news, scores and rankings updates. There are also some illuminating profiles of the top players and umpires, although the link to the player area was rather temperamental at the time of writing.

Boxing

www.cyberboxingzone.com

This US site takes a very individual view of the boxing game, producing its own list of Current Champs and Past Champs according to 'lineal' criteria, that is, you can only become a champ if you have beaten a previous champ. Every Champion at every weight since 1885 is listed, with good biographies, fight histories and fight reports for the more recent ones. There is also an Encyclopedia covering other boxing subjects from Laws and

Rules to Olympic Champions and Bareknuckle Fighters. Finally, you can read WAIL!, a monthly online journal with some good, some indifferent and some distinctly dodgy articles.

Cycling
www.bikinguk.net
This is a useful mountain biking portal with Events and Results listings from meets all around the country. There is also a well-used Chat and Notice Board area, plus links to Bike Manufacturers, Acessories, Dealers and Holidays sites.

Equestrianism
www.horsenews.com
This is a subscription-only equestrian news site from the US based International Equestrian News Network. It will cost you US$40 a year to access breaking news from the worlds of Showjumping, Dressage and Three Day Eventing. You can also receive updates on live competition from such events as the World Championships, European Championships, Badminton and Hickstead. Finally, you can access action photos, Virtual Course Walks, audio interviews, feature articles and an email newsletter.

Hockey
www.hockeyonline.co.uk
This site from the English Hockey Association is something of a triumph of style over substance. The design is slick and funky and the site is quite good for fixtures and results information from the English Hockey League. However, beyond that the content becomes rather skimpy. The England national team section was particularly disappointing with player information

limited to age, caps and club. It certainly does not inspire enough confidence to part with the £9.50 subscription necessary to join the England Fan Club.

Field Hockey
www.fieldhockey.com

Conversely, this site might be described as a triumph of substance over style. Frankly, the design is a mess, but the news service is useful and timely with daily reports on hockey matters from all over the world. The site also acts as a portal for www.talkhockey.net, the most active hockey forum in the UK.

Greyhound Racing
www.24dogs.com

This is a slick site from Wembley plc and bookmakers William Hill, which provides online live coverage of evening greyhound meetings. As well as live streaming video feeds from the track - you will need at the very least a 56kbps connection and a copy of RealPlayer before you can receive this - the site has a very good news and results service. Results can be accessed via an interactive database and there are some interesting feature articles in the news section. You can also view racecards up to 48 hours before the relevant meeting or browse through a selection of local and national tipsters. Finally, of course, you can bet to your hearts content via the online betting service.

Judo
www.britishjudo.org.uk

This the official site of the British Judo Association (BJA) and contains lots of interesting information on the history of judo, how to start judo, and how to find your nearest club. It also has a link to www.twoj.org, the official quarterly magazine of the BJA. This is a slick, professional site with well-written reports from judo championships, extensive photo galleries, player profiles, and competitions for prizes.

Netball
www.england-netball.co.uk

The official site for the All England Netball Association is rather unwieldy, but yields some useful information if you are prepared to wade through a fair few dead-end links. The best sections are England Squads, where you will find photos and brief details for current international players, and Club Search, which has (incomplete) regional contact details for players looking for a club. The forum in netball chat is well used and lively.

Olympics
www.olympics.org

The official site of the International Olympic Committee has a rather pompous tone and certainly could not be accused of taking itself too lightly. It does, though, provide a glimpse of what can be seen in the Olympic Museum in Lausanne, reveal what initiatives are being taken in the war against doping, and give a history of the Games. There are also some useful links to the official sites for Sydney 2000, Salt Lake City 2002, Athens 2004 and Torino 2006.

Sailing
www.sail-online.com

This site, of French origin, is useful for catching up on sailing regatta news and has special sections for major regattas such as the Olympics, the Vendee Globe or the Americas Cup. It also has European Weather forecasts, sections on the Rules and Strategy of sailing, and links to Rankings organisations.

www.virtualspectator.com/allsports/sailing/

Here is a fun way to follow ocean yacht racing. Virtual Spectator takes the position data from regattas and turns them into 2D and 3D simulations of the races. You can watch what happens 'live' or rewind and replay to see the whole race unfold. Current simulations include Vendee Globe, Super Cats!, the Olympics and the America's Cup. It cost $19.95 to download the 3D software at the time of writing.

Show Jumping
www.bsja.co.uk

This is a straightforward, unassuming site, which concentrates on getting information across in the most succinct way possible. There are no multimedia elements but there is a Notice Board of frequently updated news items, a comprehensive Show Calendar, ranking lists for Horses and Riders, and related links in the Information section.

Snooker
www.embassysnooker.com

This is a useful, quick reference site for catching up on latest tournament News or checking up on Rankings. There is also a list of Tour Dates with archive results and prize money details. Finally, there is a glimpse Behind the Scenes of professional snooker, including a section on how snooker is televised and a history of Riley, the cue makers.

Swimming

www.swimnews.com

This Canadian site is produced by the publishers of Swimnews print magazine and has an international flavour, despite concentrating on news and results from North American meets. The site has a minimalist design but there are good sections on Special Events such as the Olympics, World Cups, European Cups and Commonwealth Games with a full results, analysis, reports and photo service. The rest of the site is devoted to a mass of facts and figures such as World, Olympic and Commonwealth Records, Rankings, Swimnews Points Ratings Charts and Performance Analysis Charts. There is also a free email newsletter service, but the links for the Photo Library and Biographies were not working at the time of writing.

www.britishswimming.org

This is the official site of the Amateur Swimming Association and offers a useful mix of news, results, records and rankings for Swimming, Disability Swimming, Masters Swimming, Diving and Synchronised Swimming. There are also a great set of links for swimming clubs all over the UK and a strong Olympics section, which has athlete histories and biographies as well as results and photos from Sydney 2000.

shopping

overall rating:	
★ ★ ★	

classification:
cricket equipment

updated:
periodically

navigation:
★ ★ ★

content:
★ ★

readability:
★ ★ ★

speed:
★ ★

UK

www.cricketdirect.co.uk
Cricket Direct

This is a well-stocked, keenly priced cricket equipment store, with particularly good descriptions of its products. On the downside, there is no online ordering and the order process can be quite laborious – first you have to browse the catalogue and then open another section to fill in an order form. Payment is by post, credit card, or by electronic banking.

The site has a rather old-fashioned feel but is reasonably easy to navigate. Click on a main menu item on the left and then click again on the subsequent graphic to browse the catalogue. Be prepared, though, for some the pages to be slow to download.

SPECIAL FEATURES

Cricketdirect stock all of the major cricket equipment brands and always show a comparison between the Recommended Retail Price and Cricketdirect's discounted price. You will find Bats, Gloves, Clothing, Bags, Leg Guards, Guards and Wicketkeeper equipment from top brands such as County, Gunn & Moore, Fearnley, Kookaburra and Slazenger.

Good stock and good prices, but the site design and ordering processes are a little old-fashioned.

www.dukevideo.com
Duke Video

This is a great online store for any motorsport fan. Duke Video has over 1,500 titles and claims to have over 280,000 mail order customers. They accept Mastercard, Visa, Switch and American Express, and card details are encrypted. Shipping is usually within 24 hours and returns can be made within 30 days. All videos are offered in PAL VHS (the UK standard) format. The site has a clear design and navigation is via two main menus. The menu at the top of the screen has administrative and shopping Basket information, while you can Browse by Category in the menu to the left of the screen.

SPECIAL FEATURES

The homepage has details of the the Top DVDs, the Top Ten Videos and New Releases. You can also preview some videos by clicking on Video Clips on the homepage.

Video Catalogue is divided into Bike Videos and Car Videos and caters for niche as well as mainstream motorsport.

OTHER FEATURES

More... contains further sports videos, and there are smaller Books, Prints, Audio and DVD sections.

A dream video store for the motor sport fan.

overall rating:
★ ★ ★ ★

classification:
online video store

updated:
regularly

navigation:
★ ★ ★ ★

content:
★ ★ ★ ★

readability:
★ ★ ★ ★

speed:
★ ★ ★ ★

UK

sport

overall rating: ★★★★	
classification: e-commerce	
updated: periodically	
navigation: ★★★★	
content: ★★★★	
readability: ★★★★★	
speed: ★★★	
UK 🔒	

www.golf4less.co.uk
Golf4less

Golf4less is a well-stocked online store with plenty of choice within its sections. Delivery to mainland Britain is free for orders over £50 and there is a 14 day money back guarantee for returned goods. Golf4less accept Visa, Mastercard and Switch, and credit card security is provided via 128 bit encryption. The site has a clear, bold design with two ways to search the store. Either choose search from the main menu on the left and enter a product description or price, or browse through the catalogue sections on the homepage itself. You will find useful information in either About Us or Buy From Us.

SPECIAL FEATURES

Golf4less offers a little more than shopping in the Ask The Pro section. Here you will find Tuition and Tips from PGA professional Jon Haines. The product descriptions in the catalogue are very thorough and Jon Haines is on hand again to give a personal view of specific products.

The catalogue sections are Clothing, Bags, Balls, Beginners Sets, Irons, Nearly New, Putters, Sales, Woods, Wedges, Accessories, Junior, Shoes, Waterproofs and Trolleys. Manufacturers include Adams, Ben Sayers, Dunlop, Fazer, Maxfil, PGA Collection, Spalding, Titleist, Top-Flite and Wilson.

An easy to use, well-priced, online golf store.

www.kitbag.com
Kitbag

Kitbag are famous for having a vast range of football replica shirts but, in fact, their range of stock goes a lot further than that. There are sections for Football, Rugby, Leisurewear, Cricket, Kids, F1, NFL, Videos and Teamwear, and lots of clothes, accessories, gifts, books and games within those sections.

Kitbag accepts all major credit cards and card details are encrypted using the Verisign SSL (Secure Sockets Layer) Software. Delivery within the UK is free for orders over £25 and Kitbag aim to deliver inland within 24 hours of receiving your order. Returns are accepted within 30 days and payment can be made in Sterling, US$, Euros, South African Rand, or major European currencies.

The different sections of the site are called Departments and can be found in a main menu on the left of the screen. Once you are in a Department you will be able to use drop-down menus to narrow your search down to a Product Type or a particular Team. If you know which brand you want then you can Shop by Brand on the left of the homepage, or for an even quicker search you can follow the steps in Gift Selector (also on the left of the homepage).

SPECIAL FEATURES

Football There is a huge range of domestic and international replica shirts, although it cannot be guaranteed that you will be

overall rating:
★ ★ ★ ★

classification:
replica shirts, sports goods

updated:
frequently

navigation:
★ ★ ★ ★

content:
★ ★ ★ ★

readability:
★ ★ ★ ★

speed:
★ ★ ★ ★ ★

UK

able to find your club's current shirt. Your club almost certainly will be represented in the even bigger Retro Shirts section. Bags and Balls come from Adidas, Nike and Puma, plus some branded by team. There is also a good selection of Books, Games and Caps. Equipment includes Diadora and Puma gloves and shin guards. Gifts & Souvenirs contains flags, clocks, watches, gloves, ties, mugs and scarves, and you will find more clothing in Training & Leisurewear.

Rugby There are balls from Gilbert, a good selection of books and games, protective gear from KooGa and Silver Fern, flags and caps in Gifts & Souvenirs, and polo shirts and jackets in Training & Leisure. There is also an extensive range of domestic and international Replica Shirts.

Leisurewear has branded goods from Reebok, Puma and Umbro.

Cricket contains a good selection of autobiographies and the Wisden Almanack in Books, international baseball Caps, Salix and Slazenger Equipment, mugs, prints, models and posters in Gifts & Souvenirs, and polo shirts, ties and hats in the Training & Leisure. Again, there is an extensive range of international Replica Shirts.

Kids contains Climbing Frames, Outdoor Slides, Trampolines, Swings, Football Shirts, Leisurewear, Babywear and Minikits.

F1 has merchandise for Drivers – Irvine, Fisichella, Button, Herbert and Michael Schumacher. There are also Bags, Caps, Jackets, Polo Shirts, Sweatshirts and T-Shirts from Bridgestone,

as well as individual Team brands. There is a wide range of Videos and flags, models and ties in Gifts & Souvenirs.

Kitbag are the official UK supplier of NFL merchandise. You will find Balls, Caps, Replica Helmets (full size and mini), Replica Shirts and Team Sweatshirts.

Video is particularly well stocked and has individual sections for Football, Rugby and F1.

Finally the **Teamwear** department contains Nike branded jerseys for your very own team to play in.

A large, well-organised online store with the added attraction of quick delivery times and free delivery over £25.

sport

overall rating: ★★★★	
classification: bookstore	
updated: regularly	
navigation: ★★★★	
content: ★★★★	
readability: ★★★	
speed: ★★★★	
UK	

www.sportsbooksdirect.co.uk
Sports Books Direct

Sports Books Direct was established five years ago and, while it does not offer as many titles as its rival Sportspages, it does offer good discounts and delivers free in the UK. Deliveries are usually made between two and five days of making an order. They accept Visa, Mastercard, American Express and Switch and credit card details are encrypted using SSL software.

The site has a plain but effective design and is easy enough to navigate. The How to Order section provides a clear description of the ordering process. All the catalogue sections (listed by sport) can be found in the main menu on the left of the screen.

SPECIAL FEATURES

The catalogue is organised by the following sports: football, cricket, tennis, golf, rugby, boxing, walking and climbing, and other sports. Within a sports section you can browse by New Releases, Best Sellers or Coming Up in the top left of the screen or you can browse further sub-sections on the right. The book descriptions themselves tend to be rather brief. If you prefer, you can use the search section in the main menu, which allows you to search by title, author or keyword, or by football club.

A plain, but keenly priced online book store, with free delivery within the UK.

www.sportspages.co.uk
Sportspages

overall rating:	★ ★ ★ ★ ★
classification:	bookstore
updated:	regularly
navigation:	★ ★ ★ ★ ★
content:	★ ★ ★ ★
readability:	★ ★ ★ ★ ★
speed:	★ ★ ★ ★

Since its foundation in 1985, the two Sportspages shops in Manchester and London have become something of a national institution for seekers of sports literature. Their recently relaunched website looks set for similar success. They accept major credit cards and details are encrypted. Delivery is usually within two working days, shipping is charged at £2 for the first book and £1 thereafter, and returns can be made within 14 days. The site has a clean, fresh design and information on the online purchase procedure can be found in How it Works on the top right of the screen or in FAQ in the main menu on the left. Navigation is simplicity itself.

SPECIAL FEATURES

Featured sections can be found on the right of the homepage and include details of Signed Books, gift suggestions, a sports book Hall of Fame, the William Hill Sports Book Award, and Sports Studies. In the main menu, you will find weekly Top Ten Books and Videos. You can search the Books, Videos, CDs, Audio Cassettes and DVDs catalogues by sport and keyword with additional author and team searches for the book section. Particularly recommended books have special icons. There is also a range of replica football shirts.

A superb online bookshop for the sports fan.

sport

overall rating:	★ ★ ★ ★ ★
classification:	branded sports goods
updated:	regularly
navigation:	★ ★ ★ ★ ★
content:	★ ★ ★ ★
readability:	★ ★ ★ ★
speed:	★ ★ ★ ★

UK 🔒

www.sweatband.com
Sweatband

Sweatband's online store is crammed with clothes, shoes and equipment for Football, Tennis, Squash, Cricket, Rugby, Sailing and Fitness. It is also worth looking out for a special Christmas Section with additional stock in the run up to the Christmas period. All prices give a Street and a Sweatband price so you can access how much you are saving.

Payment is via a simple five-stage Secure Server Software (SSL) process, and they accept Visa, Mastercard and Delta. Shipment is usually in two to three days in the UK and returns can be made within ten days; handling charges may apply for large items.

The site has a clear, straightforward design and is easy to navigate. The main menu runs across the top of the screen just below the titles. The sub-menus appear on the left of the screen after clicking on a main menu item. Look out for the Special items in each of the main sections for further discounts.

SPECIAL FEATURES

Football Accessories include Adidas Gloves and Nike or Sindico shin guards. The Accessories General section contains everything from Steel Wire Pegs to Dubbin. Balls are from Mitre and Nike. Footwear is from Nike and Diadora, while Kids' Shoes are from Nike. Clothing is from Adidas and Nike, and Team Kit is from Nike.

Tennis Accessories include Slazenger, Wilson and Dunlop Balls, Wilson Bags, Karakal Grips and Tennis Tutor Ball Machines. Clothing is from K-Swiss, Nike and Reebok, and there are Sock packs from Asics. Footwear is from K-Swiss, Asics and Prince. There are Rackets from Dunlop, Head, Prince, Slazenger and Wilson plus a Junior rackets section, and a section dedicated to the new 2001 racket designs.

Squash Accessories include Dunlop Balls, Prince and Dunlop Eyewear, Wilson and Karakal Bags, Biobas Accessories, and Karakal Grips. Footwear is from Hi-Tec, K-Swiss, Wilson, Head, Mizuno and Adidas. Rackets are from Dunlop, Head, Prince, Slazenger and Wilson.

Cricket has a good range of goods from Gunn & Moore and Slazenger, including Bags, Balls, Gloves, Glove Inners, Leg Guards and Protection Pads, Bats, Clothing and Footwear. There are a limited number of Intersport Batting Gloves and Test Footwear.

Rugby contains goods from Gilbert and Canterbury, including Bags, Balls, protective gear, Team Equipment and Clothing. Footwear is from Gilbert and Nike.

Sailing Accessories include Gill Bags, Buoyancy Aids and Gloves. There is a large range of wet and dry clothing from Gill and Helly Hansen. Footwear is from Gill and Reef.

Fitness Portable Items are from Reebok. Larger items of Equipment include Bikes, Rowing Machines, Skiers, Stepping, Treadmills, Walkers and Weight Training machines. Suppliers include York, Delta Infiniti, Weslo, Healthrider, Mr Motivator, Raleigh, Tunturi, Marcy, Trimline, Proform and Orion. There is a selection of Polar Heart Rate Monitors in Training Aids.

OTHER FEATURES

On the home or Community page, there are a range of competitions with simple questions to win branded sportswear and equipment.

A well-stocked, keenly priced, online sports store.

www.the-pro-shop.co.uk
Pro Shop

overall rating:
★ ★ ★ ★

classification:
online golf equipment store

updated:
regularly

navigation:
★ ★ ★ ★

content:
★ ★ ★

readability:
★ ★ ★ ★

speed:
★ ★ ★ ★

UK

Theproshop claims to be the UK's largest online golf store, and it is absolutely packed with golfing products at keen prices. All items are priced in both Sterling and Euros. Theproshop accepts all major credit cards and details are encrypted. Shipping is free within the UK using the three working day option, but you will have to pay if you want quicker delivery. Returns can be made up to 60 days after purchase. The site is well organised and easy to navigate. First you can choose between ProShop and Woman in the top right of the main menu which runs across the top of the screen. You can then either browse through product categories in the coloured menu, or look at the entire Product Directory in the black and white menu just below. Administrative information is also in this black and white menu.

SPECIAL FEATURES

Closeouts is a rundown of the latest offers.

Product Directory has the following sections: Accessories, Golf Sets, Bags, Balls, Clothing and Waterproofs, Drivers and Fairway Woods, Gloves, Irons, Putters, Shoes and Wedges. The golfing equipment brands on offer include: Adams, Ben Sayers, Callaway, Cobra, Dunlop, Maxfli, Mitsushiba, Mizuno, Orlimar, Ping, Pinnacle, Strata, Srixon, Taylor Made, Titleist and Wilson.

A huge online store for all your golfing needs.